Be Good,
Stay Strong,
Love, Dad

A GenX Dad in a Digital World

Patrick McLaughlin

Quaker Press Legacy Publishing—Phoenixville, PA
Paperback ISBN: 979-8-9910276-0-1
eBook ISBN: 979-8-3302902-7-7
Library of Congress Control Number: 2024913044
Title: Be Good, Stay Strong, Love, Dad: A GenX Dad in a Digital World
Author: Patrick McLaughlin
Digital distribution | 2024
Paperback | 2024

Published in the United States by New Book Authors Publishing

Dedication

For my wife who continues to bloom in Autumn.
For my boys who simply make me proud.
For my parents and siblings who remind me.
For my friends, few and far between, but always right here.

For every father who's held their child's hand.

*Dads are most ordinary men turned by love into heroes,
adventurers, storytellers, and singers of song.*

–Pam Brown

There is nothing to writing. All you do is sit down at a typewriter and bleed.

-Ernest Hemingway

Table of Contents

Preface

When I first became a father in the mid 90's, the world was sliding head-first into the maw of an unprecedented technological eruption. Video tapes and VCRs were losing ground to the DVD. Two guys from Stanford registered the domain name Google.com on something called 'The Internet.'

The inaugural text message was sent via Vodafone in '92. It read, "Merry Christmas." If that didn't send a flare of ironic dread up your spine, you weren't listening closely enough. This was some Sky-Net level stuff, and the subsequent and perpetual seismic tremblers of technical advancement heralded a new world and nifty new ways of communicating. Those paying attention might posit a new way of living.

Now, I was born in 1965. That puts me in the first year or the fifth year of the Generation X population depending on who you ask. We have an estimated 65 million people born between the generally accepted GenX years of 1965 to 1980. I was a Northeastern, middle-class, suburban kid and there were a ton of us. We had 3 homeroom classes of 30 kids each in our grade alone at the local neighborhood Grade School. We had about a dozen neighborhoods. We had a Highschool graduating class of 1200 students in 1983. That's a lot of kids.

Our regional demographic in those days leaned toward Irish, Italian, Polish and Black. Most second generation, all working class, all pulling the plow, all products of post-war parents who understood the value of making hay while the sun shined. They worked. We worked. Everybody had a job to do. It was understood. And bitching was minimal. Why? Post Depression Era Moms. That's why. We'd get a quick slap if we even considered looking grumpy. After all, babies were starving in Africa and here you are with clothes on your back and a nice bowl of oatmeal to boot so quityerbitchin'.

It was also the end of a way of life.

The days of a household surviving on one income were screeching to a halt. The infrastructure for before and after school care and activities was not yet a thing. Our afternoons were ours. We knew where we needed to be and what we needed to do, but we had time and freedom. We had autonomy for great swaths of time. We had free air at the gas station to keep our bike tires pumped, long sweltering summers and swimming pools to hop, Slurpee cups as big as our heads, movies like Jaws and Star Wars at venues inexpensive enough to watch a dozen times in air-conditioned comfort. We had long evenings burning punks to keep the skeeters off, playing GetAway and Flashlight Tag, laughing and telling stories.

It's an easy thing to whip out the rose-colored glasses in looking back at our formative years, but we all know that life's best lessons are learned under duress. Throw 5000 hormone-ravaged kids together in a massive high-school with maybe 100 teachers and staff. This was a pressure cooker of Alcatrazic proportions. Did we fight? Yeah, we fought. I saw a Phys Ed teacher held 2 feet off the ground by his neck. A casualty of harsh words to the son of a bricklayer. This kid moved pallets of cinderblocks by hand during his summers and weekends. No doubt he grew up hearing stories about mom and dad getting roughed up by zealous teachers back in the days when authority was uncontested. Like the rest of us, he…well, he contested authority.

Even though our high school halls sometimes became Madison Square Garden, if we weren't friends by the end, we were at least civil and non-antagonistic, living to sit through another class. The girls didn't trifle either and more than once I saw torn ears being pinched together with paper towels. Fun was the norm however, even if occasional mayhem ensued.

A quick aside if you will. This is the origin of my respect

for women. I grew up with sisters and a schoolteacher Mom so I already knew the heights of nurturing and love that women can produce. I also knew the depths of malice from which they can unleash hell in many, many forms. My older sister could nail you square in the nutz with a wet tennis ball from 30 feet. And that's not a lucky guess. She probably still can but there's no way I'm giving her the shot.

Sister Ivan Koloff's three-inch punch was legendary in the 5th grade. I saw her put my man Sketties' head through a schoolroom door window with a shot to the spine from 6 feet away. Why? He was simply in the wrong place at the wrong time. You wonder why GenX lives with their head on a swivel?

Anyway, in my experience, women are the glue that keep male society from imploding into a Cormac McCarthy novel. How do they manage that? By being scarier.

Did we learn? Yeah, we learned. We learned about girls. We learned about great music. We learned about cars and booze. We smoked, fought, laughed, and passed the chew cup around the table in the cafeteria. You need a classic hallmark of GenX kid? We were older than our years and possessed an earned disdain for authority.

We were also the last kids to have dedicated student smoking lounges in high school.

"But you don't wanna sit tight you don't wanna play it cool
You don't wanna whole life like the first day at school
I don't wanna fight wars, I don't wanna die young
So don't keep saying like father like son
I can't hear you (still I can't hear you)
You make no sense to a boy like me "

News at Ten – The Vapors, New Clear Days, 1980

Our GenX upbringing is being touted as "Feral" these days. Feral is a strong word and doesn't give credit to parents or community. I would call our upbringing "Enforced self-sufficiency". If we were altar-boys selected to serve the 6AM daily mass for the 2nd week in February, we didn't expect a wakeup call and ride to church. We set an alarm, got dressed, rode our bike or walked to the church and prayed the priest was not smelling like Four Roses when we got there. In a mid-winter delirium, I once got up an hour too early and slept under a pile of cardboard boxes behind the deli next door until the church got unlocked.

The upside wasn't heaven or acclaim. The upside was dough. The pay from weddings and funerals was ours to hoard. In this, as in life, the solid performers got the choicest assignments. The choicest assignments paid the most dough.

GenX kids learned this lesson early and these so-called feral children more often than not were working at the gas station, movie theater, ice-rink or produce isle at the grocery store well before the age of 16. My father was a printer. I could clean and grease a 2-color Heidelberg offset printing press when I was 11.

Old before our time? Nah. I'd say we were the beneficiaries of early experience and early responsibility. We were, by necessity, able to navigate personalities, tempers, distances, expectations, crisis, and tragedies under our own steam. We felt the weight of those decisions personally. We learned, adapted, and thrived under our own steam. Sure, we all had casualties and missteps along the way. Some hurt more than others, but all were object lessons in how to survive.

We also had sensible generations willing to step in and guide us if we were bold enough to ask. These were generations who had seen real casualties and global missteps. GenX has spoken to WWI, WWII, Korea, Vietnam, and current war veterans in our lifetime. We listened and learned.

I had a great-uncle on my mother's side. Uncle Sam, no less. At summer picnics he would gladly let you take a gander at the sneaker-sized hole in his chest hidden under his white t-shirt. This party trick was a gift of shrapnel from the Kaiser in a German trench in the War to End All War. He had a scarred face and gravelly voice from mustard gassing. Yet here he was, with a family and a productive lifetime behind him, gleefully telling all the kids gathered around; "When God was making "Noses", I thought he said "Roses" and told him I wanted a big red one!" You wanna talk about honest grit and genuine badassery? You wanna talk about the iron structure the USA is built upon? Look no further.

GenX has a very useful talent honed to a razor's edge in our childhoods. We can absorb information and distil it down to truth or bullshit immediately. We know propaganda when we see it. After all, it was our generation who wore the threat of nuclear annihilation like a comfy sweatshirt for so many years. Our thoughts tended toward the cynical. Our goals tended toward the minimal. At the end of the day, we were just hoping to have enough money for a slice of pizza and a coke after the street-hockey game.

If the bombs dropped in the meantime, at least we knew enough not to look at the big flash when it happened.

"Let's dance in style, let's dance for a while
Heaven can wait we're only watching the skies
Hoping for the best but expecting the worst
Are you going to drop the bomb or not?
Let us die young or let us live forever
We don't have the power, but we never say never."

Forever Young – Tiffany, I Think We're Alone Now, 1984

Introduction

When my boys left home for school, one went 300 miles away to a big city university, the other to a military academy 1700 miles away. Both partings hurt and prompted a series of letters from me to them covering things that old-school Dads know but rarely discuss. Why? Men. That's why. Who trusts a chatterbox?

GenX was a wonderful, nerve-wracking, sphincter-tightening time where wins vastly outnumbered the losses. Those years created a new generation of genuinely tough, honest and productive people across the US. The following pages are a small effort to impart some of the wisdom those years generated. I am sharing those actual letters and lessons I sent to my sons. I am sharing these lessons because I see a desperate need for common sense and survival instinct in today's softening world.

I dug through old notebooks and found my original written draft of the first letter in Chapter 1. Yeah, notebooks, quit rolling your eyes. The remainder of the letters are actual emails. See how GenX adapts? No changes were made other than names/locations for privacy. That's a promise and a warning.

Do not take to heart the cussing, views, stances, digs, caustic comments and dark humor. This is just how I communicate. Not perfect but effective. These were personal letters of advice and encouragement to my boys in our own vernacular. If feathers get ruffled, that's your issue. I don't have the patience or inclination to alter and risk the authenticity of the letters. My views and statements are mine and I'll own any sagacity or idiocy. That goes for sentence structure and made-up words as well. I may have to include an actual lexicon when all's said and done. Sentence-diagramming Sister Charles Bronson from 6th Grade would be spinning around in her box.

If anything in the following chapters seems untoward, keep in mind that GenX, as a whole, tends to communicate in sarcasm, cynicism, thinly veiled threats and an unbridled, sardonic humor. We had specters of global catastrophe that overshadowed local human pettiness and we were uniting under that threat with humor that was organically diverse and available to all. Witness the golden age of television.

TV during our formative years was a mixture of Dean Martin Celebrity Roasts, All in the Family, Professional Wrestling, Good Times, The Gong Show and Soul Train. Howard Stern was on regular FM radio just hitting his profane and hilarious stride on the morning drive. Our heroes were Evel Knievel, OJ Simpson, Joe Frazer, Bugs Bunny, Rocky, The Blues Brothers, Eddie Murphy in the Red Jumpsuit talking about Bill Cosby's roo. These were different times. Can you blame us for our sarcastic bent and penchant for underdogs and dark humor?

A guy in the back wants clarification about the Bill Cosby reference.

Well sir, in the early '80's timeframe, the lovely and elusive Autumn my future wife, and I saw Eddie Murphy live at a small theater downtown. It was the red leather jumpsuit tour early on in his career. Eddie, being in Philadelphia, launched into an off-script story about he and our local Philly hero Bill Cosby together at a party in Hollywood. It was 15 minutes of Bill Cosby's private parts arriving in their own limo. Bill Cosby's private parts being Sherpa'd around the party by Gary Coleman. Bill's remarkable way with women. His ability to make their eyes roll back into their heads. It was absolutely hysterical. Definitely risky. Damning, especially in Philadelphia, but he killed. Eddie got a standing-O. It took decades for the Coz to get busted, yet his Modus Operandi was common knowledge 40 years ago. Gonna let that sit there for consideration.

Thanks for the question.

Anyway, GenX is the least socially divisive group since the Greatest Generation. Yeah, I said it. And I'll use the venue above as an example. All races, side by side, laughing and high fiving each other while one of our own got torched by one of the best. It wasn't kids versus kids back then or culture versus culture or left versus right. It was all kids versus the bloated machinery of politics and corrupt leaders and the media driven atmosphere of impending doom over which we had no control. We had better things to worry about, like having fun. After all, we were the last generation to have regular weekend high school dance mixers.

Our music was a blend of cultures delivered by blended bands of all colors and ethnicities. The Specials, Madness, Earth Wind and Fire, The Clash, The Beat, Bob Marley, Prince. We danced together. We worked together. We observed together. Our common enemy was the establishment, not each other.

"So get back to work an' sweat some more
The sun will sink an' we'll get out the door
It's no good for man to work in cages
Hits the town, he drinks his wages
You're frettin', you're sweatin'
But did you notice you ain't gettin'?"

The Magnificent Seven – The Clash, Sandinista! 1980

The sad fact is, we've lived to see the glue that held us together dissolved by artificial hatred created by that same media and promulgated by extremists on both ends.

My boys are both now out of school and particularly well-established, middle-of-the-road adults. The letters continue. I haven't decided if the letters are for my benefit or theirs, but the messages do resonate for today's crop of young people.

Why? Because being a man today is the same as being a man 1000 years ago despite what the media portrays. I believe our past generations of forefathers would smile and nod at the observations and humor you are about to see.

To the fathers young and eager, to the fathers old and wistful, former sons all, this is for you. I know you'll understand.

"Before you cross the street,
Take my hand.
Life is what happens to you,
While you're busy making other plans."

Beautiful Boy – John Lennon, Double Fantasy Stripped Down, 1981

Lexicon

Turns out a lexicon was needed after all. The jury finds that I created a whole bunch of words and actions over the years that might need a brief description. Some of these words have been in active use in our clan for decades. I'm adding the list here up front. When you run across one of the words, you'll get a small serotonin burst of recognition as a reward.

Also, check out the repeated terms if you need a heads-up as to what's coming. If you continue on this course, here there be ~~monsters~~ boys.

- Alcatrazic - big
- Balz – balls
- BarrafaLlama – toddlers' pronunciation of our former President
- Basta – exclamation, Enough!
- Beast – verb, to execute in an awesome fashion
- Boner – clown
- Boning – moaning, whinging
- Boss - adj, super cool, verb, to do like a pro
- Bozo – verb, to wander aimlessly
- Bruce Lee – verb, to quickly and thoroughly punish an enemy
- Bunger – booger, snot
- Crick - creek
- Dingus – clown
- Doofus – clown
- Do – verb, perform, execute

- Do-nuthin – noun, one who does not perform or execute
- Doogan – our dog, any dog
- Elephants – the elements, as in weather
- General Lee – automotive verb, to peel out, skid or run from the cops
- Gimbus - noun, clown, verb, to goof around
- Gold – something awesome, nod to Seinfeld
- Ice-Ball – sick feeling in the pit of your stomach when shit goes bad
- Jebus - Jesus
- McDoink's – any fast food
- Mondo – huge
- Nads – balls
- Noggin - head
- Noob – the new guy
- Nutz – balls
- Pie – pizza
- Puss – cat, grumpy face
- Pussy – effeminate clown
- The Real – a genuine article among imposters, nod to the Iron Shiek
- Roo – penis
- Sammy - sandwich
- Schlub – clown
- Screed – lengthy written or verbal monolog
- Shillelagh – Irish war club
- Skitch – to hang onto the bumper of a car surfing through snowy streets
- Snuzzles - allergies
- Spongepants – shortened title of annoying cartoon
- Spratz – verb/noun, the act and product of explosive diarrhea
- Swimps – shrimp
- The Man – The Corporation running the globe

- Toof – tooth
- Toofus - teeth
- Whinge – to cry and complain, see boning
- Wise – verb, to act wisely
- WiseAss - clown
- Wuhan Times – the pandemic
- Yam - to cry and complain, see whinging
- 'Zah – pizza
- Zorky – hurtful projectile of bent metal

So buckle up, keep your hands inside the vehicle and expect some bumps.

"I might as well go up and talk to a wall,
'Cause all the words are having no effect at all.
It's a funny thing, am I all alone?
Something has to happen to change the direction,
What little filters though is giving you the wrong impression,
It's a sorry state, I say to myself."

Words – Missing Persons, Spring Session M, 1982

Chapter 1
Goodbye

When I graduated high school in 1983, the majority of our 1200-member class went to a small handful of local but respected universities. Our college careers were geared toward Arts and Sciences and our paths usually led to local jobs. Our circles of friends held together, new friends were gathered, and the sense of community was strong. Despite politics and distractions, we recognized the timeline of "School-Work-Family-Community" as the basis of a productive life. We were working with the last remnants of the Leave it to Beaver and Happy Days paradigms. Times, they were changing.

While GenX progressed from school to work and beyond, technology continued to morph and we continued to adapt, produce, and forge our own paths. We watched the environment change and saw free time for kids turn into regulated time. We witnessed the growing pains and took notes. GenX approached parenting with what else? Practicality, execution, and a healthy disdain for other peoples' nonsense. It was a proven model by now.

My 2 boys, Charlie and Mike, were 3 years apart in age. Charlie was the eldest and Mike was a Y2K baby. They were lucky to have extended family close by and all the support a kid would need for a safe and pleasant childhood.

But this isn't about their upbringing, this is about letting them go.

As parents, do we ever know if we have given our kids the right tools to succeed? There's no rule book. There's no parent primer. There are only good intentions and hopefully the brains, the love, and the drive to direct, protect and nurture the young and growing bodies and minds of the lives we've created. That's a lot of nouns and verbs but I know we tried.

That's where this story begins, with the goodbye.

*Late Summer, 201**

Dear Charlie,

This stuff is gold, so keep it. You will be heading off to school soon and I want you to know a few things. These are likely things you've heard before, but in my experience, they are important for a smooth ride.

The best policy for peace of mind is honesty. Be honest. You'll never have the ice-ball if you are an honest person.

Socialize, have fun but be responsible. Not only for yourself but keep your friends out of trouble too. At least try….

The quickest, easiest way to derail your life is to get a girl pregnant, get a DUI, go to jail for something stupid like a fight. Don't do it. Just don't.

Cool kids don't end up making money. They end up fat and poor. Be the smart kid with good grades and an awesome future.

Work you do now will pay you back in the future with a classic car, a nice house and money to burn. Remember that when you want to stay in bed, blow off a class or drink too much. This is your job as well as an investment in your future life.

Be nice. Be smart. Be the guy that Grandmom would be proud of, every day.

You will come across dirt-bags that tell you hard drugs like cocaine, meth, ecstasy, heroin and all those synthetic, brain killing drugs are fun and harmless. No. They will kill you. They are illegal. They are no good. Not even once. Get yourself out of that situation immediately.

When you drive, you are responsible for the lives of those in your car. Driving is a job. A car is a tool. Do it right.

Keep your eyes open all the time. You will be able to spot opportunities. You will be able to spot danger and bad situations. Know the exit on an airplane. Know when a shady dude walks into the room. Know if there's a car in the lane next to you.

I heard this morning that the kid from Grandmom's neighborhood who was missing was found dead by the crick where we used to catch snakes. Shot himself in the head. His teacher sent him an email saying he was getting an F for not turning in a homework assignment. So, he killed himself.

Remember something for me. This is life. There are moments of joy and moments of shit. Surround yourself with good people who love you, and hopefully you will have more joy than shit. But there's no guarantee. Be strong and live your life. Learn to laugh at and learn from the shit. No one can beat you but yourself.

Charlie, you decided years ago that you are the boss and I'm proud of you. We don't love you because of your grades or your money or your haircut. We love you and who you are and always will.

Be Good.
Love,
Dad

This was the first letter I'd ever written to my oldest boy. It's as rough and unpolished as could be and he heard it all before, but I wanted him to hear it from me. He needed reminding. To know the responsibility of being on his own. To understand that the responsibility of being a capable citizen doesn't just mean looking out for himself but those around him as well. He needed to know he was loved and capable of success on his own merits.

For years, from kindergarten to 12th grade, whenever I saw my boys off to a new school day, my parting words were, "Remember, it's more important to be nice than to be smart." They both heard that phrase so often that it should have its own dedicated groove in their brains. My oldest, Charlie, was now heading off to follow his own path. But this time, he was in the driver's seat, and we were now in the stands watching.

GenX parents today have kids in college, almost in college or recently graduated. They will tell you that these goodbyes are brutal. They are. I'm a gnarled, grumpy, old-before-his-time cuss and every major goodbye reduces me to tears to this day. Why? It's a tough thing to bounce around a freshly empty house and see the made beds and the clean rooms, hearing…echoes.

The only thing tougher is to not have your kids at all.

This was our first goodbye, but nothing I'd ever come to master.

"It's the end of the world as we know it.
And I feel fine."

It's the End of the World as We Know it - R.E.M. Document, 1987

Chapter 2
The Rules of Drinking

The same envelope that I handed my son the day he moved into his dorm, in addition to the letter above, held a document called The Rules of Drinking. Drinking alcohol was a very accepted social norm in the formative years of the GenX population. Our neighborhoods still had the last of the 10-stool local tappys where you could walk in with a fiver and walk out toting 2 beers, 2 shots, a bawdy Irish joke and some change under your belt.

We learned to drink by swigging cold sips of cheap beer on Dad's lap at summer barbeques. Our Moms smeared whiskey on teething baby's gums and made us whiskey, tea, honey and lemon toddies when we were sick. Everybody had a bottle of Rock and Rye during flu season. We had a relative who put Crème de Menth liqueur on shaved ice sno-cones for the kids with zero irony. They were great days.

We graduated to partying in garage lofts, basements, and woods. Cheap beer and boom-boxes were the vehicles of many a momentous night. We were not operating any motor vehicles, or in shady, dangerous areas. We were in the neighborhood, with friends, hanging around, laughing, listening to music and stories and passing around whatever we were fortunate enough to scrounge up. A lot of us didn't drink at all and nobody cared.

This was a gentle slope for a kid becoming familiar with booze. We all, to various extents, knew alcoholics, had them in the immediate or extended family and saw their impact on people and peace. We had a workable dynamic to our social drinking. We would start strong then throttle back. We knew the long game. Get out, see friends, have fun, make it home, avoid trouble. We were teens with the routines and sensibilities of 30-year-olds. If you want a responsible kid, give them responsibility and the freedom to accomplish.

Sadly, that freedom was given away to play-dates, before and after school care, camps and organized sports stifling the opportunity for kids to explore things on their own. No longer was there any gentle slope for kids to learn about the accoutrements of adulthood. One day they are shooting hoops in the driveway. The next day they are signing a lease and managing a class schedule, roommates and unlimited parties with God-knows-what drugs and alcohol.

I felt the need to distil my thoughts and experiences about drinking. Yeah, I said that too. I needed to give my kids not just perspective about drinking, but practical instruction about the application of drinking. Thus, were born my Rules of Drinking. It's been massaged a bit over the years. Friends and co-workers have asked for the Rules as their own fledglings study the great beyond.

What you see here seems to be the final iteration. Again, this is solely *my* observation and *my* commentary delivered in *my* language to *my* boys. It may be patently incorrect or spurious, and it's definitely incomplete, but it was and remains an effective primer.

THE RULES OF DRINKING

1. **Doesn't matter what the rest of them are doing, do what you want to do.**
2. **Keep count of what goes in and when it goes in.**
3. **Manage your time. Are you driving? You need 3 hours to clear a breathalyzer.**
4. **Eat a big, greasy meal before you start drinking. It will delay the absorption.**
5. **Different booze has different effects. Know how it will hit you.**

6. All booze will kill you if you drink too much. It takes far less than you think.
7. 2 drinks in 1 hour makes you illegal to drive.
8. 5 beers and 5 shots in 1 hour may kill you.
9. Drunk? Put a trash can next to your bed. Sleep on your side so you don't drown in your own puke. It killed Hendrix, Cass, Belushi and countless other people.
10. College students die every year from booze, and not just from car accidents.
11. Never, ever mess with a drunk girl. Stay away. If they need help, enlist a female to help.
12. Never be alone with a drunk girl.
13. If someone calls you a pussy for not doing shots or stupid drinking games it's OK to laugh at them when they are sitting in their own piss.
14. Drinking is not a game. It's a skill and an art. Games like quarters and beer pong are for amateurs.
15. You can appear to be drinking all night yet be totally sober. Water looks just like vodka.
16. Some people prey on drunks. They will wait till you are alone then kick your ass and steal your stuff. Keep your eyes open, not just for yourself but your friends too.
17. Never leave a drink unattended at a bar or party. Weirdos will drug and cornhole you.
18. Know where you're drinking and who you're drinking with. Have an ally and an escape plan.
19. Pick a drink early and stick with it for the whole night. Mixing drinks will make you sick.
20. Drinking will make you look and sound stupid. Know your limits and pay attention.
21. Drink water as every 2nd or 3rd drink. Hydration will keep you from getting too hung-over.
22. Never, ever drink on an empty stomach. That's

begging for a disaster.
**23. You have alcoholics on both sides of the family.
Don't make it a habit.**

So, behold The Rules. They may come across as paranoid propaganda, but in my experience, carnival barking gets noticed. The target audience here were my boys going away to school. If the written equivalent of a Three Stooges ear twist and noggin rattle was necessary to get the point across, so be it. Why? Because I'd much rather have informed, inexperienced, drinkers on the alert instead of on a stretcher being toted out of some frat house stairwell by paramedics or, worse yet, in a courtroom.

First I drank the whiskey, then I drank the gin
I tried to make the toilet but I broke my fucking shin
The next thing that I knew I was in London in the rain
Staggering up the platform on the boat train

Boat Train – The Pogues, Peace and Love, 1989

Chapter 3
Doesn't Get Easier

The next goodbye came a few summers later. Now, a bit of background information is required. Our boys, by the grace of God and genetics and McDoink's Chicken Nuggets did well in school and enjoyed sports. Our eldest was now pursuing dual degrees in Business and Biology with a minor in Informed Drinking.

Unbeknownst to us, our youngest had started the year-long process of applying to a US Military Academy. We were not even aware Mike had applied until he needed a ride to the State Capitol where a formal grilling with a US Senator and Army General were scheduled to take place. Why? Boys. That's why. Read to the end if you're considering getting one of your own.

So, in true Mike fashion, he was awarded the rare appointment. In true Mike fashion, he waited until the last possible day to accept just in case something better came along. The weeks leading up to my young son's departure for the Academy were difficult. He was a grumpy bastard. The lovely and elusive Autumn my wife called it "Soiling the nest", which turns out to be an actual thing. I called it a supreme effort in self-control. The government would've hated if I killed him after all that rigmarole. Hopefully an actual boot in his ass wouldn't disqualify him.

We were doing our best to keep a positive face forward while internally wondering what the hell we/us/he/them just agreed to pull the trigger on. We were not a military family. More importantly, Mike was a brick-head. If he didn't want to do something, he didn't do it. When he did want to do something, he did it until he won. Competitive? Sheesh, in a house full of Alphas, including our doogan, Mike was a force to be reckoned with.

We were hoping and praying he really, reaaaaaaally wanted to do this.

The day came for the drop off. And yet again, we found ourselves in the stands.

*Late June, 201**

Hey Mike,

Just saw you get sworn in on the parade field. Me and mom were dead in front of you in the stands. Hope you could see us. We did a big "Go Mike!" at one point when it got quiet.

I like your Commander. We spent time with her at the parent meeting after you got on the bus. She has her head right.

Uncle Ted called and said he is very proud and knows you will kick ass. He said that you "get it" and know the screaming, pushups and shit are all part of a very calculated process to get everybody's head out of their ass and work as a team. Stuff you are very familiar with and good at.

He also said you won't get a better, more rigorous, world class education than where you are right now. He literally said, "EFF the Ivy League, they're a bunch of privileged Pus$%# with more money than brains. Mike's going to run rings around those As#$%H^%s in a few years."*

I put him on the mail list so you should be hearing from him.

Anyway, hang tough. We're heading to the airport today knowing you are in great hands and ready for the challenge and the opportunity to lead and succeed.

Looking forward to hearing your stories when the summer's over.

Stay Strong.
Love,
Dad

Wow. This letter seems so positive juxtaposed with the reality of that day. I had just watched my kid get on a bus knowing he would have his phone taken away, get sworn into the US Military and roll right into basic training within days. He would have no contact with the outside world for 8-12 weeks. We could write him letters, using their email to mail service on-base, but there was no guarantee he would receive any of them any time soon. Talk about flying blind. This was also the first appearance of the Stay Strong, Love, Dad closure. He'd be seeing that a bunch.

*Late June, 201**

Hey Mike,

Very interested to hear how things are going. I can only imagine. Hope all your gov issue clothes fit good.

Of course, the measurements were taken by a professional. She got that inseam twice :-D

Try to keep cool and sunscreen your dome. I'm sure you're killing it out there with the parade rests and the right faces and such.

Remember, if you suck in your gut, you'll disappear, so don't scare anybody.

Eat, sleep, get screamed at. Just like home. I know you will do well.

Stay Strong.
Love,
Dad

If you're sensing some desperation in that cheery little chunk of bullshit above, you're not wrong. I knew this kid. It would either be a walk in the park, or they'd be flying him home on ConAir.

I decided he needed a "Gold" letter, like his brother

received. You'll see some carry-over, but you'll also see the mods and maybe a little polish from the years in between.

Another trait of GenX; if it's working, don't mess with it.

*Early July, 201**

Dear Mike,

I know my handwriting would totally annoy you, so I'm typing this. I'm excited that letter writing is encouraged at the Academy because I have always written better than I talk.

You are now getting settled at school. It may be a school with extra physical requirements and extra rules and uniforms and traditions and a guaranteed job at the end, but it's still a school and it's far away. It's the step your mother and I have been trying to prepare you for your entire life. It's a big step. It's going to be scary. It's going to be weird. It's going to be tough. It's also going to be fun. You will meet people and do things that are far beyond what we've ever experienced.

What I am telling you here is gold. So, keep this letter and read it from time to time when you need it.

Always remember the best team you will ever belong to is our team. Me, Mom, Charlie and the Doogan love you no matter what. Anyone in our family, grandparents, cousins, aunts, and uncles would drop everything immediately to help you. So, if you are feeling alone, remember that we have your back. You will never be alone. You will always have our love and support.

Remember that you come from rugged people, hard workers, and fighters. You have the brains, the strength, the humor, the kindness, and the grit to be a true leader. You are already a success. A success in academics and a success in being a good person. You have a long and exciting road ahead with trials, failures, and more success along the way. You haven't peaked, not by a long shot.

Stay honest. It's the single best policy to maintain your peace of mind. You'll never have the ice-ball if you are an honest person. If there is a problem. Tell people. You should never try to bear the full weight of an issue. If your grades are sucking, don't stew and sweat, get help. If you are hurt, get help before it gets worse. If you are troubled by something, anything, talk to someone about it. People never turn down a request for help. Don't be the boner who's too proud to ask.

Be honest with your timeframes. Don't procrastinate. Honesty allows you to sleep soundly. Honesty goes hand in hand with responsibility.

So be responsible. I know the Academy is geared toward this, but still, socialize, have fun, but be responsible. Not only for yourself, but for your friends as well. Keep them out of trouble or at least try. Help them when they need it. Your brother has been a great role model for you. He's a helper, he's a leader. He knows the rules. You need to know them too.

The quickest and easiest way to ruin your ride is to get a girl pregnant, get a DUI, do drugs or go to jail for something stupid like fighting. Don't do it. Just don't.

Be nice, be smart, be the guy Grandmom would be proud of. All the time.

You will come across dirt-bags in your life, even in the Academy. They will tell you that hard drugs like cocaine, meth, ecstasy, heroin and all those synthetic brain-killing drugs are fun and harmless. No. They will kill you. They are illegal. They are poison. Not even once. Get yourself out of that situation immediately. You are too valuable for that bush-league bullshit.

Drugs are dark room you can't get out of. It's best never to enter the room.

When you drive, you are responsible for the lives of those in the car. Driving is a job. A car is a tool. Do it right. I'm very proud of your driving skills.

Keep your eyes open all the time. I've taught both you boys to be able to sniff out nonsense and bullshit from a mile away. You will be able to spot opportunities. You will be able to spot danger and bad situations. Know the exit on an airplane. Know when there's a car in the lane next to you. Know when a shady dude walks into the room. Know when you need an escape plan. Know when an opportunity is being presented. Know when a person in authority has an agenda. Keep your eyes open. Enlist help from someone you trust when you need it.

You are ready for this. You've beasted everything you've decided to get involved with. I don't expect that to change. You are a super smart kid, but more importantly, you are good and kind. A smile will get you further than a 100 on a test. Every time. Keep in mind, every person you encounter has a story and is struggling with something in life. Even the people in charge. Be helpful and be kind. If your smile or cooperation lightens a person's load, they will remember you and they will lighten your load when the time is right.

Remember something for me. This is life. The moment you are in is the real world. It has always been that way. There are moments of joy and moments of shit. Surround yourself with good people who love you and hopefully you will have more joy than shit, but there's no guarantee. Be strong and live your life. Try to learn from the shit and laugh at the shit. No one can beat Mike but Mike.

You decided years ago that you were going to succeed. You have succeeded and I am proud of you. We don't love you because of your grades, or your sports or your haircut. We love you because you're you and we always will.

So go out there and do your thing. Do it with excellence and respect. Do it with humor and brilliance. Do it with a smile. I envy your adventure. Remember we are out here with you wishing you only the best of everything always.

Stay Strong.
Love,
Dad

And there went our youngest, off to follow the path of his choosing. Crazy, turbulent times for everyone involved. Our boys, our sole focus as parents for 20 years, were now distributed across the country. Our house was empty. The wee Doogan was wondering where everyone went. Yet the world rolled on like nothing happened.

"How can I just let you walk away?
Just let you leave without a trace."

Against All Odds – Phil Collins, Against All Odds, 1984

I decided at that point that I'd keep an open communication line with my boys through emailed letters. It didn't matter if I got a response, in fact, responses were rarely encouraged. These guys were busy with school and life, but if I had an opportunity to reach out with stories, news, insights, and funny stuff, I would do it.

Until then, it was…

"Just the two of us.
We can make it if we try.
Just the two of us
You and I."

Just the Two of Us - Grover Washington, Jr., Winelight, 1980

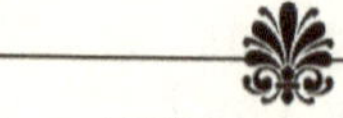

Chapter 4
Life on the Outside

Remember that time when you found out your kid was still alive?

*Late July 201**

Mikey!!!

We got your letter yesterday! Damn the mail is slower than balz. I really hope you have been getting our letters. I've been writing daily. We think about you all the time. We love seeing the pictures. We saw you doing the high dive in the pix last night. You look jacked.

Anyway, your letter sounded great. You sounded positive. You are excelling with some stuff and working on other stuff. All as it should be. Glad to hear you can manage a quick dump as needed. Very glad you are getting fed and have protein shakes to pound. Take advantage of the shakes.

I was very happy to hear you are making connections with some of your squad. Very happy to hear you are already leading in some capacities. It sounds like an environment you can adapt to and thrive in. I'm excited for you and very proud of you. Hang in. You are kicking ass.

The Doogan is good. I played sock ball with her yesterday until she refused to get up anymore then gave her belly rubs. I took her for a 5am walk this morning instead of working out. She took 2 big whizzes and a massive on the other side of the loop.

We're between hunting seasons and the fireworks have

stopped, so she's getting back to her normal self. She misses you too.

So, these 12 kids and their coach in Thailand were exploring caves on a team trip and got caught in a flash flood and washed deep into the caves. They somehow were located, all alive, huddled on a small rock shelf 3 miles into the cave. Pitch dark, surrounded by water. The only way out would require scuba gear. They were starving, dehydrated, hypothermic and running out of air.

Anyway, 2 weeks later, they are all out and alive. One Thai Seal rescuer died on an oxygen resupply run over the weekend. Unbelievable story of grit overcoming bad luck.

So, when you think you are having a shit day. You could be on a rock shelf 3 miles underground, in the dark, cold, hungry, running out of air and waiting to die.

Anyway, we loved getting your letter. We hope you are getting ours in a timely fashion.

Keep up the good work. I hope the days are flying by.

Stay strong.
Love,
Dad

That was the response to one of 4 letters we were to get from Mike in his 4 years at the Academy. About what I expected. He was settling into the environment, doing well and we were fine picking at what scraps we could get. So here we are with Charlie pushing through the last semesters of college. Here we have Mike in his first semester of college. We had weathered the goodbyes!

*Fall, 201**

Hiya Charlie!

I've written a bunch of letters/emails to your little brother including the #1 written letter and the Rules of Drinking since he's been away. They are probably a boring pain in the ass for him, but it seems not quite fair that you only got the 1, 3 years ago. So, now you're on the radar.

Number 1, I love your room downtown. AC, food, Wi-Fi, new bed, clean sheets. I'd be hanging in there loafing every chance I had. Enjoy it. Just keep the goddam shitter clean.

Here's an excerpt from the letter I sent your little brother today. It's about you:

Mike, here's a quick story about your big brother. He txtd me yesterday pissed off. The A&S School will not honor his Ireland trip as international credit because the program was part of the Business School. He was counting on that being the last of his required international credits and not having the trip count would put him in a seriously bad way possibly extending him another semester.

When he heard this on the phone with the admin, he asked for her manager's name and number, because he knew this needed fixing right away. (the fact that he called the dept at all just to make sure the credits were in place is a testament to his boss-hood) Anyway, he got a call 1/2 hour later from the manager. She told him she dug deeper and found that they will indeed accept his Ireland trip as the international credits that he needed.
He asked for documentation.
He called me back letting me know it was all ok.

Never be afraid to step up to the next level if you are not getting what you need. It usually will shake stuff loose.

Anyway, you are the boss, Charlie. You think about things the correct way. You know what you need to do in order to get the results you want. Most people your age, or any age for that matter, don't think strategically. They just bozo along and bitch when shit doesn't swing their way.

I'm very proud of the way you handle yourself, like an effing man. Keep it up. It will only be a huge benefit in your career.

You've been a great example to your little brother, and I appreciate that. He saw you up studying late, handling assignments, participating in clubs and sports and being a solid citizen. He followed right in your footsteps and owned that school when you handed off the baton. He's heard your college stories and knows it takes work and planning and dedication to do well in that environment.

He doesn't miss much, and you have definitely gotten his mind right when it comes to schoolwork. He's also heard your stories of dealing with assholes and drunks and I am sure, when the time comes, he will perform like he knows he should.

Anyway, thank you for being you. Keep up the good work.

Be good.
Love,
Dad

"So what becomes of all the little boys
Who run away from home?
The world just keeps gettin' bigger
Once you get out on your own."

On The Nickel – Tom Waits, Heartattack and Vine, 1980

Chapter 5
Wisdom

The lovely and elusive Autumn my wife made an executive decision that she would take point in assessing the health and well-being of our remote progeny. For that to happen, she needed to see their faces. By decree, she implemented a Sunday morning video call when Charlie went away to school. Once Mike got his phone back and was free to communicate, we added him on. This was a pure GenX move, assessing what available tech would assist the family unit and making it serve.

The Sunday Call has persisted across years, time zones and countries. The assessments continue and our personal connections are renewed and strengthened. What started off as a potential chore has become a respected and anticipated event for all. Our last call gathered our family together from Geneva, New Mexico, London, and Pennsylvania.

Another quick aside if I may, again about women. The executive order organizing this call was issued in a clarion of such sovereignty, that no living thing within earshot would dare attempt aught other than complete and immediate subjugation. Birds flew from the trees, and all fell silent. Rarely did the lovely and elusive Autumn my wife, exercise her powers of ex-cathedra, but when she did, she was indeed infallible. Why? Because the lovely and elusive Autumn my wife, is a GenX female.

She and I dare say the entire crop of GenX females, have an earned understanding of how to be ruthlessly effective, imperious, and rock hard, when necessary to reach their chosen endpoint. They'll put beans on the table. Don't ever doubt they'll make you eat 'em, too.

GenX females also know the limitations of the male species

like they issued a handbook. How? They probably issued a handbook.

Anyway, The Sunday Call was an excellent decision and one in a long history of excellent decisions handed down by the lovely and elusive Autumn my wife.

Mmm - but it's poetry in motion
And when she turned her eyes to me
As deep as any ocean
As sweet as any harmony
Mmm - but she blinded me with science
And failed me in geometry

She Blinded Me with Science - Thomas Dolby, The Golden Age of Wireless, 1982

Ok, back to business. The boys are well into the routine of school. The parents are back into the routine of work. The Doogan is sleeping.

My letters begin to take a 'Things to Think About" direction. Since most of my own personal mental meanderings would never withstand actual scrutiny, and shame on you if you think otherwise, I decided to include the mental meanderings of other people. Tips to make life easier. Ideas to keep you out of trouble. Lessons learned the hard way, so they don't have to. In short, wisdom minus the pain.

*Late September, 201**

Hiya Charlie,

Happy Thursday. Another steamer with big thunderstorms in the afternoon. We got an hour or so of big rain and thunder last night. The wee doogan was in her bag extra early.

Great stuff with your job activity list. It is a lot of work, but it will pay off in the most unlikely ways. I am proud of you.

Stay focused and great things will happen.

Uncle Ted bagged out of our mountain weekend. He has some unforeseen court appearance that messed him up. Which blows, I was looking forward to the weekend. I may head up on my own anyway. I need to empty the plumbing before the freeze sets in. Plus, the new mattress for the big bed is being delivered today and you can't leave those things rolled up for long or they get weird.

Anyway, here are some cool thoughts from the Irish. Remember your Irish and Viking roots and be proud.

One of the theories surrounding the financial, political, social, and global success of the US is thus: It takes huge balz to pack up all your shit, uproot your family, immigrate and settle in a strange new country. It takes motivation, a desire to work hard and confidence that you'll be successful.

Anyway, the US was founded and populated by these types of people. From everywhere. They built a powerhouse of a nation. Ireland is a tiny place, but the Irish immigrants and descendants infiltrated every position of power in the US very quickly right up to President.

Alternatively, Australia was founded as an enforced penal colony. They introduced cane toads to eat sugarcane beetles then realized toads can't climb and are now overridden by both. Then they built a 1500-mile wire fence to keep rabbits out of Western Australia, failing to remember that rabbits were built to dig holes. They recently unleashed a biological, respiratory disease targeted at the expanding bunny population....we'll see how that works out.

Here's some thoughts from your ancestors:

Is obair latha tòiseachadh
Translation: Beginning is a day's work.

Nach gorm na cnuic a tha fada bhuainn
Translation: How green the hills which are far from us.

Cuimhnich air na daoine às an tàinig u
Translation: Remember the people from whom you came.

Abair ach beagan's abair gu math e
Translation: Say but little and say it well.

Bu mhath an sgàthan sùil caraid
Translation: A friend's eye is a good looking-glass.

Breac à linne, slat à coille 's fiadh à fìreach – mèirle às nach do ghabh Gàidheal riamh nàire
Translation: A trout from the river pool, a staff from the wood and a deer from the moor - thefts of which no Gael was ever ashamed.

Is sàmhach an obair dol a dholaidh
Translation: Going to ruin is silent work.

Chan fhaigh an duine socair nach fhuilinn dochainn
Translation: A person who cannot suffer pain will not find comfort.

Lìonar beàrn mhór le clachan beaga
Translation: Great gaps may be filled with small stones.

Théid seòltachd thar spionnadh
Translation: Cunning overcomes strength.

Thig crìoch air an t-saoghal, ach mairidh ceòl 's gaol
Translation: An end will come to the world, but music and love shall endure.

Be good.
Love,
Dad

Going to ruin is silent work. Lordy, ain't that the truth.

*October, 201**

Hiya my Charlie,

Your weather looks like a nice couple of days, cool and sunny! Hope you're keeping warm, sleeping well, eating good and finding some happy times during the day.

Here's some wisdom from Ernest Hemingway. You know him. You read his stuff. He was a great writer, soldier, professional adventurer, fisherman, boozer, and brawler. You were on his boat, The Pilar, down the Keys. He settled down there when he got old, wrote, and fished. Not a bad life, but he was an unstable bloke who ended up blowing his own head off with a shotgun. Shows you can have it all and still not be happy. Happiness is a choice. It makes life nice.

- *Man is not made for defeat.*
- *There is no friend as loyal as a book.*
- *The best way to find out if you can trust somebody is to trust them.*
- *The world breaks everyone, and afterward, some are strong at the broken places.*
- *I like to listen. I have learned a great deal from listening carefully. Most people never listen.*
- *There is nothing to writing. All you do is sit down at a typewriter and bleed.*
- *Always do sober what you said you'd do drunk. That will teach you to keep your mouth shut.*
- *We are all apprentices in a craft where no one ever becomes a master.*
- *Never mistake motion for action.*
- *As you get older it is harder to have heroes, but it is sort of necessary.*

- *Happiness in intelligent people is the rarest thing I know.*
- *Wars are caused by undefended wealth.*
- *Time is the least thing we have of.*

Be good.
Love,
Dad

GenX recommendation: The Florida Middle Keys. Beautiful, tropical locations, in the US, where people mind their own business.

Leave Key West to the cruise ships and bar crawlers. Head north of No-Name Key or south of Key Largo for the real Keys experience. You may never come back. If you find Skinny, tell him I said Yo.

*Late November, 201**

Hiya Charlie,

Hope you are back into the swing. This is an important semester. Take care of yourself physically and mentally. My boys are stalwart and smart but bad shit is right around the corner so always keep your guard up.

Here is some wisdom from one of Philadelphia's original homeboys, Buffalo Ben Franklin.

- *An investment in knowledge pays the best interest.*
- *It takes many good deeds to build a good reputation, and only one bad one to lose it.*
- *To succeed, jump as quickly at opportunities as you do at conclusions.*
- *Either write something worth reading or do something worth writing.*

- *Diligence is the mother of good luck.*
- *It is the working man who is the happy man. It is the idle man who is the miserable man.*
- *Distrust and caution are the parents of security.*
- *If you would be loved, love, and be loveable.*
- *When in doubt, don't.*
- *He that lives upon hope will die fasting.*
- *Do not fear mistakes. You will know failure. Continue to reach out.*
- *Employ thy time well, if thou meanest to gain leisure.*
- *Blessed is he that expects nothing, for he shall never be disappointed.*

Be good.
Love,
Dad

Above is a tenet which is sadly overlooked these days but cherished by GenX. Franklin says, "When in doubt, don't." In our unsupervised travels and adventures growing up, we learned to listen closely to our guts. We saw everything and our brains picked up even more. Call it your sub-conscious, call it your guardian angel, call it intuition. To Gen X it is a real and routinely exercised superpower.

We can smell 'hinky' a mile away. We can spot lies as they emerge from the source. We can sidestep an altercation or projectile vomit or a car beating a yellow light just before it happens without fail. How? Our radar is always on, and we are wise enough to listen. Again, Franklin nails it saying, ***"Distrust and caution are the parents of security."*** Founding Father Franklin, welcome to a working tenet of GenX.

*Early December, 201**

Hi there my Charlie,

I hope you are doing good. Looks like you might get some snow today. We're in the 20's all day according to Dave's Ultimate Double Doppler Triple Whiz-Bang Weather Screening Fogramis that's correct 12% of the time.

So in this hectic time of pre-xmas, I've decided to impart the peaceful wisdom of the ages in the form of quotes from Buddha. Yo, Buddha.

Gotta hand it to the old Asians. They knew how to wise.

I wouldn't have listed them all, but shit, there's not a clinker in the bunch. Take your time with these and consider.

- *Endurance is one of the most difficult disciplines, but it is to the one who endures that the final victory comes.*
- *People with opinions just go around bothering each other.*
- *Believe nothing, unless it agrees with your own reason and your own common sense.*
- *Even as a solid rock is unshaken by the wind, so are the wise unshaken by praise or blame.*
- *You yourself must strive. The Buddhas only point the way.*
- *Ardently do today what must be done. Who knows? Tomorrow, death comes.*
- *If you propose to speak always ask yourself, is it true, is it necessary, is it kind.*
- *Silence the angry man with love. Silence the ill-natured man with kindness. Silence the miser with generosity. Silence the liar with truth.*
- *Nothing can harm you as much as your own thoughts unguarded*
- *No one saves us but ourselves. No one can and no one may. We ourselves must walk the path.*
- *We are what we think. All that we are arises with our*

thoughts. With our thoughts, we make the world.
- *Peace comes from within. Do not seek it without.*
- *As you walk and eat and travel, be where you are. Otherwise you will miss most of your life.*
- *If your compassion does not include yourself, it is incomplete.*
- *A generous heart, kind speech, and a life of service and compassion are the things which renew humanity.*
- *Meditate. Live purely. Be quiet. Do your work with mastery. Like the moon, come out from behind the clouds! Shine.*
- *What you think you create, what you feel you attract, what you imagine you become.*
- *Your work is to discover your world and then with all your heart give yourself to it.*
- *Kindness should become the natural way of life, not the exception.*
- *Being deeply learned and skilled, being well trained and using well spoken words: this is good luck.*
- *Do not dwell in the past, do not dream of the future, concentrate the mind on the present moment.*
- *When watching after yourself, you watch after others. When watching after others, you watch after yourself.*
- *The secret of health for both mind and body is not to mourn for the past, not to worry about the future, not to anticipate the future, but to live the present moment wisely and earnestly.*
- *Buddhas don't practice nonsense.*

Dag, I might be a Buddhist. I love these quotes. There's some very good stuff here. Some should resonate with you. pay attention and keep them in mind.

Be good.
Love,
Dad

Wisdom. It's a small word with big meaning and a myriad of interpretations. It's a big world out there. We have ages of written wisdom and infinite schools of thought. Much has been lost over time, but we still have Google's worth of insight accessible at our fingertips. I enjoy other people's wisdom. They have experienced that which needed to be documented so the future might understand and benefit. From Marcus Aurelius to Dr Seuss to The Iron Sheik. It's free, it's insightful, it's funny, it's stupid, it's simple and brilliant. It's a window into the human mind of the times.

"Every hundred year, mother make baby like Iron Sheik, Michael Jordan and the Jesus. Only one chance to prove you are the real in a lifetime." - The Iron Sheik

I enjoyed inflicting other people's wisdom on the lads. It was an effort to not only expand their view of the human condition but to show the similarities of disparate cultures across eons of time. Why? Because people are people, were people, will be people and will build and burn as people have always done.

Barring or even despite a cataclysmic event, future disparate cultures across future eons of time will be doing the same simple shit they have always done. If my boys could learn a little something from other people's experience, wins and losses, it would be worth a shot. It was a free primer in the quest to be The Real.

"And after all the violence and double-talk
There's just a song in all the trouble and the strife
You do the walk, yeah, you do the walk of life
Hmm, you do the walk of life."

Walk of Life – Dire Straits, Brothers in Arms, 1985

Chapter 6
Requiem for a Tube

GenX had to deal with the explosion of digital technology like no other. As kids in the 60's and 70's, we were the remote control of the day getting up on parental command to change the console TV knob between the 6 or 7 available channels that were broadcasting. PBS for Sesame Street, Zoom! and The Electric Company. ABC, NBC, CBS for news, soaps and Mike Douglas. WTXF for Ultraman and Dark Shadows. WPHL for Speed Racer, local sports and the epic and hilarious GenX version of Bandstand, DOA. Dancing on Air.

TV's didn't get stolen back then. Why? Because you would need 4 guys, a forklift and a panel truck to make your getaway. Who among us doesn't have a permanently swollen knuckle from those inch-thick, hardwood console lids dropping onto our hands? Hell, it was an actual sport back in the day.

We were the generation that coveted our older siblings' stacked stereo systems and massive speakers playing the latest Cheech and Chong album. GenX saw the rise and fall of the 8-track, cassette tapes, boom boxes, Walkman's, CD's, IPods, Bluetooth and Alexa. Now we're back to albums it seems.

As practical GenX consumers, we tended to avoid jumping on technical bandwagons until the inevitable bugs got worked out.

A guy in the back wants an example.

Well Sir, allow me to submit this sentimental illustration wrapped in a rare "Boyz" letter to both sons.

*Winter 201**

Hello my boys,

Here's the saga of the new flat screen that now anchors the TV room. It all started before Christmas when several family members, having been exposed to the wonders of high-def, LED, 4K, wide-screen, digital, WIFI integrated flat TVs began to whinge about our trusty, giant, square-tube TV. Our giant TV that we built the house around. We dedicated an entire wall and 5 huge pieces of furniture to 190 lbs. of solid-state technology. 'Murica.

Both you boys sat on my lap in front of that old TV. We would play 'Whomp'. We would play blocks with letters, numbers and animal names. We would play 'Ninja Finger'. You can both thank me later for your cat-like reflexes and nerves of steel. We watched the World Trade Centers Collapse, Saddam Hussein get captured, BarrafaLlama get elected. We watched Littlefoot and Teletubbies and Sesame Street and Arthur Duncan hoof his way across the screen on many quiet Saturday nights.

We watched Jeopardy. We watched old movies where the cowboys talked like New York gangsters. We watched new movies. We watched Super Bowls and Phillies in the World Series and Doc and Chooch work out a perfect game. We watched snowstorms with the fire going and blizzard wind whistling outside. We watched VCR films of your old birthday parties, early Christmas mornings when you'd stumble down the back steps following a trail of Hershey Kisses toward piles of loot.

We've had that TV about 7300 days. Figure a minimum of 3 hours a day and that old TV gave us about 22K hours of, if not entertainment, at least diversion. It was a workhorse. It outlived 2 dishwashers, 2 refrigerators, 2 washers, 2 driers, 2 broken arms, 1 broken leg, 1 home heating system, 4 cars, 1 garage door opener, a kidney stone and 2 water heaters. It survived the rise and fall of VCR's, CD's, nerf darts and worked well into the digital age. It still was working when I unplugged it.

I wonder if it knew its demise was at hand. I wonder if it was sad. Does a machine that is built to transmit information have the capacity to absorb information?

Did the TV watch us? If so, it would've seen a lot. It would've seen you, Charlie, toddle around your infant brother while the puss cozied up next to him on the floor. It would've seen you guys dance, fight and laugh over 1000 different things. It would've seen you both grow into big, strong, smart kids, then men. It would've been proud when you went from answering 0 Jeopardy questions to just about beating your old man, but not quite. It probably wondered why you, Mikey, liked Spongepants so much when he was played out after Season 1.

The TV didn't want to move. It took work just to pry it away from the wall. It repeatedly fell off the dolly in a bid to stay in the house. It fought tooth and nail to stay out of the car. It fought harder than a north pacific halibut and beat me up worse. It left me with a sore back, crushed finger and pulled bicep. Finally, exhausted, it rolled onto its short side and slid into the back of Mom's car with a sigh of defeat and the groan of stressed vacuum glass, calcified circuit boards and petrified plastic housing. I'd like to think it was relieved and not sad and confused. Tough to tell.

Taking the swinging doors off the TV cabinet gave me a solid 39 inches of width. A 44" flat screen is 38 inches across. BJ's was having a sale, I had a long weekend. The stars went into alignment and a new upstart now graces the family room. It's bright, it's clear, it's light. The sound is crisp. The wires minimal. It's an upgrade in quality, a few steps toward minimalism. It remains to be seen if it has the soul of its predecessor.

One thing can be certain. This new TV will not cast its digital glow upon anything remotely as spectacular as the journey you guys have taken under the watchful gaze of the old TV.

RIP old friend.

Love,
Dad

"Remote control to change the station,
But that won't change your situation.
Have you seen what I mean?
I'm a little gnome that's in your dreams."

Remote Control – Beastie Boys, Hello Nasty, 1998

Chapter 7
Wednesdays

Mike once bounded into the kitchen from the yard where he was goofing off with his friends. It was likely 8th or 9th grade. I was in the kitchen eating his lunch snacks. Anyway, his arm, at the elbow, was pointing in the absolute wrong direction. I mean backwards. Had to have hurt like a bastard.

He goes, "I think I broke my arm."

I looked at him and stifled a gag, "Jesus shit. Ya think?? Get in the car."

What followed was surgery for a blown apart left elbow complete with plates, screws, and months of rehab. Sports and fitness being a major concern of Mike, he was a model rehab patient. More importantly, he needed to have the reconstructed joint manually stretched every day. If not, he would lose considerable range of motion and risk other growth complications. "A painful process," they said. Scared the crap out of us.

For years, when the boys were only small, I or the lovely and elusive Autumn my wife would wake them up for school. I woke them up on Wednesdays with a short rhyme from a song they enjoyed as babies.

"Well, I know today is Winds-Day
And this is how I know
It is always on a Winds-Day
That the winds begin to blow!"

A Rather Blustery Day – Sterling Holloway, The Many Adventures of Winnie the Pooh, 1977

This wake-up routine was long over, but here I was again, waking up Mike in the dark to get his arm properly stretched for the day. I reinstated the Winds-Day wake-up recitation the very first time Wednesday rolled around. It was a familiar comfort during a not so pleasant time. The early-morning grump-factor was in play. The pain factor affected both stretcher and stretchee.

But we worked that arm. And we worked that arm.

Through the sheer brick-headedness of all parties involved, today he's got excellent motion and mobility. We sent a picture of him flying through the obstacle course in basic training to his surgeon with a heartfelt Thank You.

God bless modern medicine and the people that deal in healing. They are so often unappreciated for the miracles they perform.

Now with Mike being away, at a military academy, hip deep in grueling physical and mental pursuits, again I reinstated the Winds-Day wake-up recitation in his letters. Why? It was a familiar comfort during a not so pleasant time.

*July 201**

I know today is Windsday and this is how I know, because it's always on a Windsday that the winds begin to blow.

Hiya Mikey,

It's work from home Wednesday. Nice out. Saw you trying on dress uniforms and hats last night on photog. You look like a pro. Time is ticking down to survival at Joe's Plateau. I bet that will be cool. 10 people to a tent is what I hear.

Probably will have porta-potties.

Here's what you need to know about those things. The blue juice in them splashes up when you drop a turd from 15 inches. They call it the blue burn. It'll make you sick at worst, uncomfortable at best.

What you need to do. Number one, bring sanitized handy wipes if you have them. You'll need them for your seat, your ass and your hands and maybe to stuff in your nose. Number two, heh, number two, make a landing pad of toilet paper to catch your dump. That way it won't splash on you. Then you can make another pad on top to help it sink so the next guy isn't inspecting your diet.

Today Trump is meeting with NATO. He's telling them the days of the US footing the huge majority of the NATO expenses and initiatives are over. He wants everyone to pay and stop draining our dough. Great stuff.

You'll be missing Lil G's Sesame Street Wing Ding 2nd B-day party on Saturday. Everything else is quiet and hum-drum. You'd be sprawled out watching the Jokers if you were home with nothing to do, so count yourself lucky.

Once you get past the next couple of days, you'll be doing some new, cool stuff. Hang in!

Anyway, I am proud of you. You are a great kid and a force to be reckoned with. The world will be your buffet to choose from soon. You are getting set up for big victories, just continue to put the initial work in and enjoy the moment. I want to see some smiles from your tired face.

Stay strong.
Love,
Dad

*August 201**

I know today is Windsday and this is how I know, because it's always on a Windsday that the winds begin to blow.

Hiya Mike,

It's Wisdom Wednesday, Viking Style. There are some great ones. I like to think about the lives these guys led that gave them this insight. Having this knowledge and not having to go through the shit they did for a hard-earned truth is a great thing.

Read, ponder and assimilate.

Too much ale and a man's heart is laid open for all to see.
~The Saga of Olaf Haraldsson

Better to fight and fall than to live without hope.
~Volsunga

Ill is the result of letting fear rule thine actions.
~The Saga of Harald Hardrade

Where wolf's ears are, wolf's teeth are near.
~Volsunga Saga,

Kinsmen to kinsmen should be true.
~The Saga of Olaf Haraldsson

Fear not death for the hour of your doom is set and none may escape it.
~Volunga Saga

When men meet foes in fight, better is stout heart than sharp sword.
~Volsunga

Often times it is not numbers that wins the victory, but those who fare forward with the most vigor.
~The Saga of Thrond of Gate

With many who come to power and honor, pride keeps pace with promotion.
~The Saga of Magnus the Good

No one is a total fool if he knows when to hold his tongue.
~Grettir's Saga

Ill it is to abandon honor and integrity in exchange for injustice and greed.
~Bandamanna Saga

It is an old custom for the wisest to give way.
~The Saga of Harald Hardrade,

A person's actions are often worse than their intentions.
~The Saga of Hrafnkel Freysgothi

When truth and fairness are different from what is law, better it is to follow truth and fairness.
~Bandamanna Saga,

A person should not agree today to what they'll regret tomorrow.
~Bandamanna Saga

He falls not whom true friends help forward on his way.
~Egil's Saga

Stay strong.
Love,
Dad

*Mid July, 201**

I know today is Windsday and this is how I know. Because it's always on a Windsday that the winds begin to blow.

Hiya Mike,

3 days till you march into the woods. Sure you will enjoy the change of scenery.

Some good news. Mom's big project is not being sold. They are keeping the asset and giving her the lead role in final development and marketing. 4 to 6 years of extra work and nice coin. Very nice lucky break. We'll be able to visit you a bunch.

In other news. Doogan's in her bag. She told me it's hot out, then told me to go away.

Charlie's having wings with Cousin Tiny tonight at Wheelahan's. Dwayne the Rock Johnson's new movie 'Skyscraper' cost 160 million to make and has made a whopping 9 million on its opening weekend. He's put out 3 movies in 3 months, all the same hero/disaster genre. Hello, overexposed.

I see some kids in masks on photog. Try not to get some sickness. That would blow. Heard one kid got sent home for surgery because he blew out his bellybutton doing sit-ups. No shit. Quit laughing. Herniated protruding naval requiring immediate surgery. They said he will have auto acceptance next year if he wants to come back. Lesson here....stay tight. No blowouts, pink socks or 4-inch outies.

We did get some stuff from Schreyer. He's having a team building thing and your subject is the Little Mermaid. Dead serious. No joke. They expect you to contact the team and join their on-line group to brainstorm about the big show. It's next month. Yet another reason to stay tight.

Like the old Indian told Josie Wales. "Endeavor to persevere."

Here's a wee puzzle.
There was once a recluse who never left his home. The only time anyone ever visited him was when his food and supplies were delivered, but they never came inside. Then, one stormy

winter night when an icy gale was blowing, he had a nervous breakdown. He went upstairs, turned off all the lights and went to bed. Next morning, he had caused the deaths of several hundred people. How?

Stay strong.
Love,
Dad

Mike got accepted into a large State College's Honors program. It was his Plan B. He refused to turn them down until he completed basic training. Smart move having an escape plan if the Academy pushed the wrong button. The Honors Program was sending him all kinds of fluffy stuff for team building. Meanwhile he was involved in a different team building exercise crawling through barbed wire, getting gassed and shooting machine guns. He did eventually turn the Honors Program down. The recluse was a Lighthouse Keeper.

*August, 201**

I know today is Windsday and this is how I know. Because it's always on a Windsday that the winds begin to blow.

Hiya Mike,

It's work from home Wednesday! Pouring rain outside. Weather continues to be gross. Looks like you guys are having similar rain squalls and storms minus the humidity and excessive heat. You're generating your own heat, no doubt.

    Mom's taking some visiting big-wig out to dinner tonight so me and Charlie plan on going somewhere. I'll let him pick. His work is boring. He broke up with Matilda (again). He's got to move back downtown in a couple weeks for back to school. He's kinda bummed.

Senior year at college is a very weird time. You're supposed to be past your hardest classes and able to relax. However, you're also expected to know what you want to do and get a job doing it, which is very stressful. That, on top of moving into an off-campus house, the wacky girlfriend, having a car in the city, his paper and presentation due at work, the new course schedule, is all weighing him down.

I'm going to tell Charlie the same thing I told you. Just take small, manageable bites until the situation is all eaten up. Nothing on his list is life or death. It just seems so. He'll be fine and do great things. But it feels like a lot is expected of him right now. You're feeling the pressure too, I know.

The work you're putting in right now is a total bitch. But, it is setting you up for success. The discipline and stamina they are making you grow today will be strong tools for the academics coming up. The academics are going to be rigorous and take effort, scheduling and follow-through to do well.

The stuff Charlie's worrying about now, housing, car permits, class schedules, interview clothes, post grad employment, are all things you will have under control. Which is great. Stay the course and keep kicking ass.

There's definitely light at the end of the tunnel. By the time you get this letter, you'll be 75% done with basic!

We are very proud of your progress.

Stay strong.
Love,
Dad

Parents day finally rolled around. We travelled out to the Academy and had a nice visit with Mike. He looked sharp, happy, healthy. He was killing it. We had avoided the ConAir scenario.

*September 201**

I know today is Windsday and this is how I know, because it's always on a Windsday that the winds begin to blow.

Hiya Mike,

It was so great to see you. You look great. You look happy. You have extremely cool clothes. You have good grades. You are staying very active by necessity. I think you are settling in very well. Me and Mom think about you and Charlie all the time. Literally.

We know about Charlie's trials and victories because he is easy and vocal about them. You have always been rather taciturn ever since you were wee about your daily stories. We always had to pry information out of you about school, friends, sports and stuff. You were always easy and vocal about grades and tests and teachers.

Anyway, now that you are in a remote location like your brother, we would love to hear about you personally, more than your grades. The story of your lid and the hacky sack was easily my very favorite moment of the trip. Number one, it was funny as balz. Number two, it was a clear moment of victory and boss-hood for you. Number three, it showed you can recover from a mistake and have a group of comrades around to witness and celebrate.

Plus, "Sack" is possibly the coolest call name of all time.

While we were in line at the Southwestern gate at the airport, the Parents Group lady was talking to us. You know, the one married to the Marine. She said she saw you at the football game surrounded by girls, having a great time. The Marine looked at me and winked, and said, "He's doing juuust fine!"

Anyway, that story made me happy. I know you are strong; I know you are smart, I know you are ambitious and motivated and a friggin monster when it comes to the execution of anything. (except getting rid of the sticks in the back yard)

What I wonder about is how you are doing personally with friends, being part of a group, forming bonds, etc. Those are the things that will make life happy and bearable and especially fun. You probably have it wired, but we don't know. If it's a struggle, we don't know. You've always made friends on the field and in the classroom and you know how it works. People (especially the people you knew at school) as a proven historical fact have loved you and thought you were awesome and felt you were a leader.

We would just like to hear the stories and know you have a social network to lean on and talk to. We would love to know you are happy with your decision to be where you are. We would sleep better knowing you are happy, period. Because, if you're not, we would both burn the world to the fucking ground to get you what you need or where you need to be, to be happy.

So, I know it's weird to have to talk about stuff, especially with your lame-ass parents, but let us know how it's going. Life where you are right now is unlike the life of 99.99% of the freshman out in the world. I'd like to hear about it, hear how bad it sucks, how great it is, if you are good, if you are struggling, if something's funny or sad or just plain eff'd up or boring or hard. Fill us in.

Stay Strong.
Love,
Dad

No doubt you're dying to hear the hacky sack story and it's worth repeating. Maybe it will cancel out that weak, annoying whine I hear emanating from that letter above. Geeze 20's Dad, pull your shit together. You weepy bastard.

Anyway, new Academy Cadets are broken up into groups under a senior student officer. Mikey's group Number 21 had just finished a particularly grueling part of the survival course and were relaxing somewhere. When the break was over, they gathered their gear and headed out. Somewhere along the trail, Mike discovered he left his hat behind. Uh Oh. "Control of your cover" is a big thing.

The senior officer must've researched the backgrounds of his squad because he knew Mike was a fan of hacky sack. When Mike approached the leader to go recover his cover, the officer threw him a foot-bag and said the price for recovery is 21 kicks in a row without a drop. The crowd gathered round and started counting. Mikey, being Mikey, calmly and expertly performed 20 consecutive kicks and whistled the final 21st kick over the officers' head by a scant few inches. The squad went wild, and Mike got a new call name. Sack.

*Mid-October 201**

I know today is Windsday and this is how I know, because it's always on a Windsday that the winds begin to blow.

Hiya Mike,

Hope you are having a good week.

Here's some old wisdom from Miyamoto Musashi. He wrote The Book of Five Rings in the 1600's. He was the king of the Japanese swordsmen, a Ronin during the feudal days in Japan. He had over 60 duels and never lost. Wrote the book when he was old. It is one of the most revered writings about strategy in existence. All of these quotes are his from the book.

- *"It is necessary to know ten thousand things by knowing one well. If you are to practice the way of strategy, nothing must escape your eyes. Reflect well on this."*

- *"Respect the gods and Buddhas, but do not depend on them."*
- *"You must cultivate your wisdom and spirit. Polish your wisdom: learn public justice, distinguish between good and evil, study the ways of different arts one by one.*
- *"When you cannot be deceived by men you will have realized the wisdom of strategy."*
- *"There is nothing outside of yourself that can ever enable you to get better, stronger, richer, quicker, or smarter. Everything is within. Everything exists. Seek nothing outside of yourself."*
- *"It may seem difficult at first, but all things are difficult at first."*
- *"Step by step walk the thousand-mile road. Study strategy over the years and achieve the spirit of the warrior. Today is victory over yourself of yesterday; tomorrow is your victory over lesser men."*
- *"In strategy it is important to see distant things as if they were close and to take a distanced view of close things."*
- *"Consider yourself lightly; consider the world deeply."*

Stay strong.
Love,
Dad

There are a lot of Wednesday letters but I'm wrapping up with Musashi. As a GenX kid and a father of boys and a boy myself, I have seen some epic wipeouts. I mean, like bounce 3 feet off the ground, lights out wipeouts. I've witnessed and experienced blood, busted bones, flawless uppercuts and unexpected exits from trees and cliffs. Boys like to move. They move fast and haphazardly. They move with commitment. They move with an endpoint in mind, but they rarely consider consequences.

Strategic thinking is a necessary skill to keep them out of trouble.

A guy in the back is asking for an example of commitment without forethought.

Well, Sir, off the top of my head. There was a time when we were in between houses. Our first house sold fast; our new house was not yet available. The parents of the lovely and elusive Autumn my wife allowed us to move in for the time necessary. This was pre-Mike and Charlie was a mobile and curious 3 years.

Now, between work, daycare and our temporary housing, there flowed a respectable creek. Digby Crick. In the '70's and 80's, Digby Crick was wilderness. I and my friends would often ride our bikes down to the crick in the summertime to catch frogs and snakes and swim and find the occasional Playboy if we were lucky. The area is much the same today.

After picking up Charlie from daycare, I was never in any particular hurry to get back to our temporary home so we would snug the car into some bushes on the side of a back road and slip onto the secret path down to Digby Crick. Charlie and I would wander the banks and the paths in the late afternoon sun discovering cool stuff. We'd notice the differences of how deep water flowed and looked. We'd notice how the shallow water moved, how the rocks sat and where it was safe to cross. We saw black squirrels and tadpoles and poison ivy and nettles. Outstanding decompression for a kid and a dad with an educational bonus.

One day we came upon a 3-foot green and black garter snake sunning herself on a flat rock. It looked like a painting. She must've just shed her skin. Very pretty and shiny. Charlie ran up to that snake like it was on a low shelf at Toys R Us. He snatched her up behind the head and turned to me to celebrate. I gotta admit, it was a slick grab, but the snake was almost as thick as his wrist.

As garter snakes are wont to do, she proceeded to wrap

herself around the boy's wrist, forearm and bicep smearing him with extruded noxious garter snake stink, hoping to be dropped. Charlie however, held the creature out at arm's length in a tight freeze like he was being electrocuted and wouldn't let go. You want it. You got it. Toyota. Now what?

Well, once I stopped laughing, I pulled the cotton, draw-string bag I kept in the car for exactly this purpose out of my back pocket and safely transferred the snake from his arm to the bag. Why? Boys. That's why. What's real fun without some risk? All three of us cleaned up and celebrated on the ride home.

The in-law's neighborhood, to this day, certainly has the healthiest population of snakes in the area due to our serpentine resettlements. My rationalization: it was funny and who likes rats anyway?

Charlie grabbing that snake is a good example of moving fast with commitment and not considering the consequences. Luckily it was not a Copperhead or Rattlesnake even though the chances were very slim. He had the will, the attitude and the hand-speed to accomplish his mission. His strategic planning and results just needed slight tweaking. Not bad for a toddler.

Musashi would've told him, *"All things are difficult at first."*

The Iron Sheik would've told him, *"Pencil has eraser because it make mistake."*

"You come on with it, come on
You don't fight fair
But that's okay, see if I care
Knock me down, it's all in vain
I get right back on my feet again."

Hit Me with Your Best Shot – Pat Benatar, Crimes of Passion, 1980

Chapter 8
Travels with Charlie

Where Mike was straight up facts, figures and action, our firstborn, Charlie, was all of that but with an added element of thoughtfulness and compassion for the world and his fellow man. It was a very alien concept for the likes of meself, but Charlie is nice. He enjoys people, music, hiking, nature and racking up National Park visits while travelling for work. He would enjoy my oddball reveries and musings. If I sent this stuff to Mike, it just would've made his eye twitch.

*Early October 201**

Hiya my Charlie,

Happy October. It's my favorite month of the year. The angst from school starting is over and kids are settled in the routine. The year starts to wind down and business gets less hectic. The nighttime comes earlier and I can hear the owls hooting when I take the trashcans up. The sky gets higher and clearer as the weather starts to come in from the north bringing cooler, drier air. The leaves start coming down and wood fires are lit in the neighborhood that smell so good.

We can open the windows and air out the summer stale air throughout the house. The doogan gets happy again and runs around like a gimbus in the backyard. Orange boxes of Sweetzles are back in the Acme. I can play in the garage without sweating my balz off.

Instead of 'Springing Ahead' we 'Fall Back' and gain an

hour of sleep. I love this time of year.

Anyway, we'll be heading to the airport tomorrow to go to this pseudo-family wedding in Sonoma CA. Not looking forward to travelling (or the wedding), but we have a nice little place right on the quaint town square, walkable to everything, and 3 days to relax. Hopefully the weather's good and we can get a whole bunch of steps in. If I see anything cool, I'll pick it up for you.

Good luck this week in class and all of your other activities.

Be good.
Love,
Dad

Early October

Hiya Charlie,

Happy Tuesday. I hope it's cooling off in town for you. It's still friggin disgusting here. 80 and humid. It feels like it's been August all goddam year.

I'm tired of everything smelling like damp asscrack.

We had a good trip to Sonoma CA. We stayed in this little hotel right on the town square. 6 rooms in the hotel. We stayed in 'Baxter's Room'. Named after the owner's dog. We were able to just park the car for a few days and meander around the town drinking wine and hanging out.

One night we found an Irish Pub called 'Murphy's' down an alley. There were about 30 folks flown in from Ireland for a wedding. They were singing songs and generally out of control. It was a blast. I got a few tall Smithwick's in me and ended up singing 3 songs for the crowd. They were going nuts. The mother of the groom ended up sitting on my lap when Mom went to the bathroom.

Mom was slightly pissed, but, a great night overall.

Anyway, enjoy the fall leaves and the breeze during your birthday month.

Keep your nose to the grindstone and do well, my bud.

Be good.
Love,
Dad

Allow me a small interjection here. THAT was a great night. So nice to party with professionals.

"She had lovers by the score, every Tom and Dick and Harry,
She was courted night and day, but still she wouldn't marry.
And then she fell in love with fellow with a stammer,
When he tried to run away, she hit him with a hammer."

In the Town of Ballybay – Tommy Makem, The Makem & Clancy Concert, 1977

*Late October 201**

Happy Birthday Eve Day Charlie!

22 years is a good age. You're smart, healthy, good-looking, educated, and motivated. You've got the world by the balls my man.

You've proven to be a good decision maker, a diligent student, a careful driver, a good son to your parents and most especially, a nice guy. You've made me very proud. I envy you the adventures you will have, the people you will meet and the money you will spend and the things that you'll see.

Think of it this way. When I started my job out of college, Secretaries were sitting at a front desk, typing letters on a typewriter, mailing shit through the USPS, talking to people on rotary phones, reading daily newspapers, pumping leaded gas and reading road maps. My first car was a 1975 Ford Maverick. I paid $1600.00 cash for it. Gas was 75 cents a gallon.

The crazy run of technology in those 30 years has been astounding. Shit, I watched the Apollo 17 lunar landing on a black and white TV rolled into our grade-school homeroom.

Anyway, the tech wave is not stopping, and you'll be seeing some cool stuff along the way. I think you've learned from your parent's frugality and Uncle Stan's enthusiasm not be an early adopter until the bugs get worked out. But just wait and see the flood of AI in the next 10 years, the self-driving cars, and whatever else the hell they pull out of left field.

There also will be huge developments in brain killing recreational drugs. Probably from the frigging Chinese and moved through Mexico like everything else. You've done a great job not getting involved with that shit. Keep it up. The business world was loaded with more people doing more drugs than school was. Cocaine was bigger than God in late 80's early 90's. I never got involved because I knew I would like it too much. I watched those boners come and go nowhere.

Bottom line is nobody pays big bucks to a clown. The good coin goes to the guy with a smile, a clear head and a plan of action.

So stay on the good path my bud, get your grades, get your diploma and get on with a great life. Have a great birthday weekend, stay out of trouble.

We'll see you at Thanksgiving.

Be good.
Love,
Dad

*10/31/201**

Happy Halloween!

Hi Charlie,

Looks like Trump was in your neighborhood yesterday for the synagogue shooting. Like I said in a letter earlier this year, there are dangerous assholes everywhere. You never know when they will appear with their fucked-up agenda and loaded guns, or bombs, or bottles of acid to toss in your face. (this is starting to get more and more popular in the UK)

So now and always, keep your guard up and your eyes open. Wherever you might be, know the escapes, know your potential weapons at hand, know what structure is handy that will stop a bullet. The answer to that last one is...not much.

A 9mm bullet can go through 12 sheets of drywall. Sofas, bar tables, bars, car doors, house doors, refrigerators all won't stop shit. A backpack full of books might help. Your best bet is to get the eff out, low and fast.

Anyway, statistically all this is a long shot, but if it happens, the people with a plan win. The people baffled and paralyzed get killed. It's just a smart way to live. As you were growing up, everywhere we went, I was aware of the surroundings and had an escape plan. If I didn't have a weapon on me, I knew where I could grab something and I know how to put someone down hard and fast if they come in close. Maybe I'll do a letter on that information later.

The closest I ever came, luckily, was that little dufus robbing the Pathmark near DeMarco's Pizza. He caught my eye moving unusually fast, pulling a shotgun from under his pea-coat, yelling and firing into the air. I left my cart and eased behind a pallet of soda cases when he ran by on his way to the office safe. Then I went the opposite direction through the butcher shop in the back, gathering people along

What can I say? GenX operates on a worst-case scenario mind-set. We had to be prepared for all eventualities. After all, it was just us and Swayze saving the US from an invading Moscow and Havana in 1984. Every weekend, we'd hear "WOLVERINES!!!" echoing through the woods with playing kids pouncing on opposing forces.

GenX knew the woods. We knew the shortcuts. We knew the meeting places. We knew the hiding places. We knew the train schedules and the sound an oil tanker makes rounding the blind corner of a gravel road. We knew how to build and bank a bonfire to disperse the light and the smoke from prying eyes. We knew the woods in every season. We knew when quiet fell. We knew the woods in the dark.

Today, if we were inclined to hide from our kids, our kids at any age, they'd never find us. GenX knows how to disappear. Disappearing was pretty much our daily marching order from adults. There were also so many more kids in circulation back then. No phones, no media, no destination in mind. Whether travelling in a pack or on our own, we were the lords of all we surveyed and had the skills to prove it.

We knew fire and explosives. Black Cat firecrackers, M80's, bottle rockets, those black snaky things, sparklers, punks, white, twisted paper snappers packed in sawdust. Once Disney World opened, we had neighborhood kids returning from Florida with bags of this stuff we couldn't get at home. Life was good. I have a giant brick of firecrackers right now sitting on a shelf in my house. Waiting for the right time. Why? Boys. That's why. They should come with fine print. But they don't.

By third grade we'd all had our first cigarettes. Usually in the woods. We lamented when they stopped making strike-anywhere matches because we all had the skill to pop them with our thumbnails and squint at the sky a la Clint Eastwood while sparking up a Pall Mall purloined from some mom's nightstand. I never became much of a smoker but the scent of a freshly lit Marlboro Red puts me right back onto a sun-dappled log in the woods near the train tracks in the mid 70's with Kate and Quack and a box of real matches.

And if anybody bothered us? Well, we recognized the true value of a stick and could Bruce Lee the piss out of you. I've seen it done to actual applause. We also knew one 'Whoop!" from an encroaching police car meant "Move Along." while a quick series of "Whoops!" from an encroaching police car meant "Run!" They were cool that way.

GenX's old-school war craft skills are also on point. In school, it was all fun and games until you had a zorky embedded in your ass-cheek. A "zorky" being a piece of metal paperclip folded into a > shape and propelled by a rubber band held between thumb and forefinger. BB guns were for rich kids and not very concealable anyway. We developed sniper skills with the tools at hand. At a family cook-out, I witnessed my cousin put a zorky through a robin's eye from 15 feet away much to his own and everyone else's amazement and shock. Then he got whacked by his mom and sent away.

We were the generation of wrist-rockets, pump-up water missiles, clackers, rusted steel lawn darts, wooden bats, field hockey sticks and tree forts that were legit forts. We could deal and we could also take a hit and stay in the game. We had our shorts set on fire by 2 story stainless steel sliding boards and doused them in Superfund creeks. We had our teeth punched through our lips attempting see-saw tricks. We could hit an electrical line with a tennis ball let alone your face with a crabapple. Superior skills care of epic WireBall tournaments. We wandered junkyards, hopped trains, skitched on the rear bumpers of '72 Chevy Malibu Classic Station Wagons in the snow and could evade the cops like Houdini. Hot afternoons playing Chink against a concrete wall had our hand/eye coordination and endurance honed to a razors edge. We were formidable.

The groups of GenX kids traversing the realms between schools, pizza joints, railways, ball courts, woods, fields, parks, skating rinks, malls and arcades were all aligned. Aligned in freedom and fun. It may seem like an exaggeration, but we knew some kids from any group we ran into. We knew them from schools, work, neighborhoods, churches and sports. Our groups grew, shrunk, morphed and carried on with all the common engineerings of a self-governing society. Our overseers were busy. We could handle ourselves.

No matter the neighborhood, we had everything in common. Everyone watched the Friday night line-ups on TV. Everyone watched The Wide World of Sports. Local professional sports were televised or on AM radio. Kids listened to the same 2 or 3 FM Radio Stations and heard the same music and new releases together. We all had the same lame teachers, parents and expectations. We knew the deal. We shared the same boat.

GenX was a very effective unit whose seemingly reckless exploits were actually tempered by equal amounts of caution and consequence. We needed common sense and the skills to get back to our jobs and see another day.

Unfortunately, these days we are doing a disservice to our kids if we do not educate them on violence and protection. They need to recognize and know how to escape sticky situations and people. They need to know what might provoke a whack. They need to realize TV fights are not what real fights look like. They need to know a real bullet is a powerful, frightening sonofabitch. The world's taken a disappointing and scary turn. I believe we all need the capacity to make Bruce Lee a verb again.

*Winter 201**

Hiya my Charlie,

It's a Monday. Monday's blow. Modern industrial man is conditioned to work for a certain amount of time with the reward of some time off. It's a relatively new concept. You can thank Henry Ford.

For most of mankind's history, every day was taken up with the work of surviving. People filtered naturally into their roles. Green thumbs gardened and grew, hunters hunted, builders built, fighters fought, simpletons were embraced by the whole and assisted or drew pictures in the dirt and became revered oracles.

From our perspective today it seems like an awesome way to live, but the reality probably sucked balz. Bugs, disease, other tribes stealing your people and shit, weather, starvation. We went from fire and caves to the internet and heated seats in your car. It is a crazy fast technology revolution in the grand scheme of things.

So here's a piece of wisdom from an old guy who's done the 8 to 6 grind for 32 years.

Understand what you're good at but also understand what makes you feel good inside. Understand what motivates you. If you include these 2 factors into your future plans, it will make a difference.

If you are motivated and skilled in what you decide to do, going to work everyday will be less of chore. You might not enjoy it every minute, you won't be able to control every aspect, but it may feed you personally and hopefully professionally. It should even give you opportunities to expand and grow and sharpen your skills.

It takes time to filter naturally into your role. It takes patience too. That's where education and society can help. They give you the time to understand your strengths and direction. It will probably take a few attempts to find a role that fits you naturally. It might happen right away. The lesson here is, just be aware of what makes you feel happy and fulfilled as a person and strive for it.

Most people allow life to just wash them into a space with no insight or forethought or self-awareness. Those are the ones living for the weekend. It's a pretty shitty routine.

Me, I did it halfway right. I can read people naturally and understand their perspective and motivation intuitively. It's my skill. I was also motivated by money more so than other things. Understanding this put me into the recruiting world where I interviewed candidates and companies, understood their needs and put them together for money. The job is good and the money turned out great.

My real love is in writing but the fear of not being able to pay the bills with writing led me to different things. There's no regrets, just observations and the occasional, 'what if'.

So, it's Monday. Monday's blow. For some people way worse than others. My wish for you is to have the desire to explore your strengths and motivations, the patience to let the process unfold, the wisdom to recognize opportunities and the luck to find a job that you enjoy doing every day. The King knew the deal. You gotta pay to play.

"Growing up on the plantation, there in Mississippi, I would work Monday through Saturday noon. I'd go to town on Saturday afternoons, sit on the street corner, and I'd sing and play." - B. B. King

Be good.
Love,
Dad

A quick aside if I must. I love The Blues. I had the privilege to take the lovely and elusive Autumn my wife and both boys to see B.B. King several times at small venues before the Greatest Bluesman of All Time took his place beside Muddy, Pinetop and Lightning'. Why? Living history. That's why. GenX had the opportunity to learn from the past and recognized greatness. We didn't tear it down. Life's tough enough already and the blues will tell you why if you pay attention.

GenX on employment? We're nothing if not practical. Do what you love? Not if I'll have to live in a van down by the river, pal. As the Bard of the Klondike, Soapy Smith said, ***"If you ain't gitting, you're gitting got."*** I'd suggest everyone read that again.

So, a career later, patience turns out to be a virtue, and you happen to be reading the "What if?" Why? You gotta pay to play. Even Franklin was on board saying, ***"Employ thy time well if thou meanest to gain leisure."***

Mid October

Hiya my Charlie,

It's raining like balz here again. 45 degrees and cloudy.

How'd you like that picture of Pop in the Air Force? So, him and all his Upper Digby buddies joined the AF Reserves in the late '50's to early '60's. Not exactly sure why, but it was a giant party. He tells the story about how they all had to pile in one of their cars and drive down to VA or FL or somewhere for training. One guy was so hung over they had to stop every few miles so he could run out and spratz in a field.

He remembers posing for these pictures how they had to scrounge around to find some missiles then look like they knew what they were doing and try not to laugh. He did basic at the Alamo in TX. Says it was hot. They'd give them salt tablets so they wouldn't lose water. Doesn't sound too healthy.

They called up Pop's reserve unit when Kennedy was on the verge of blowing up Cuba when the Russians began building missile siloes there in October of '62. Kennedy actually handled the situation extremely well, there's a whole movie about it, Khrushchev agreed to remove the missile sites if US agreed not to invade Cuba. Pop's unit stood down. Kennedy was shot in '63. I was born 2 years later.

Doogan says hi. She's eating like a wolverine gearing up to grow her winter coat. Her summer coat is all over the place. Her thing these days is to come and stand next to you and not move until you give her a good scritchin. Must be itchy work shedding and growing. Heh, wee doogan.

So there's 4 full weeks between Thanksgiving and Christmas. That'll be half fun, half work with finals and projects and Ho-Ho's and Holiday cheer. I'm sure downtown looks nice at Christmas time.

They say the period between Christmas and Spring Break is a drag and a dark, cold slog. What they don't realize is our DNA thrives in dark, cold, dreary conditions.

Our ancestral make-up is built around accomplishing tasks in inhospitable conditions. The Irish and the Vikings had to fish in February in the North Sea to live, chop firewood in snowy forests with wolves breathing down their necks, they had to live on root veggies and the occasional deer.

They also sat around their cabin fires and told stories, sang songs, drank tea and ale and produced some of the greatest minds in human history. So don't worry about wintertime. That's my time, that's your time. Those guys from South America, the islands, other warm parts of the world. They're the ones who cry when the sun goes away and it gets chilly. Not us.

Our clan, we put our noses in the wind and breath deep knowing the spiders and skeeters are dying, the wolves,

*bears, and big cats are in their dens, and when we're done
our work, a snug fire, and hot cup of tea, and a good book
are our reward.*

*So hang tough. You're doing great and we're proud of
you.*

Be safe.
Love,
Dad

"Life is too short to have sorrow
You may be here today and gone tomorrow
You might as well get what you want
So go on and live, baby go on and live."

Tell It Like It Is – Heart, Tell It Like It Is, 1981

Chapter 9
Happiness

This is just a wee chapter, but the information is a neat and accurate encapsulation of the GenX outlook on life. The Vietnam War was the soundtrack of our evenings around the TV when we were small. Our teens were a mixtape of nuclear proliferation, global threats, local gas shortages and grainy footage of scary Russian missile parades and high-stepping North Korean soldiers. All of this we had zero control over.

Our everyday lives were pretty damn good despite the potential for violence from on-high. Our 'big picture' was bleak but the reality of our daily classes, jobs, weekend meanderings and recreation beat the news we were hearing, hands down. I believe we had more fun just to spite the government and media clowns who were gaming with our futures.

The attitude was "Ok, world, you keep up your unproductive nonsense, we're out here quietly executing a better plan under your gin-blossomed noses and it's not scary at all."

Take a look at the people in control today. It ain't GenX. Our decrepit forebears are hanging onto power with both mummified hands in a literal death grip. Why? They know we see through their rapidly cooling bowel movement of self-serving policies and broken messages. We need to keep throwing snakes into their backyards.

GenX understood that happiness was under our control while the angry businessmen, invading Huns and howling protesters on the nightly news could manage their nonsense without us. I wanted my boys to understand how nice that could be.

*Winter 201**

Hiya my Charlie,

Hope your test went well. Good luck.

So, I got a letter from my friend Declan. He's the guy who lost his eldest son too soon. He works in a library and is putting together some sort of class or presentation on grief. He remembered something I wrote years ago about happiness and wondered if I had it.
   Anyway, I couldn't locate the original piece but wrote this for him. It's only my perspective but something to consider.
   Check it out and take it to heart.

Love,
Dad

Happiness
Comes in snippets. In moments. Vignettes of quiet observation. It's rarely found in bombast, commotion or planned event. It secrets itself in personal spaces. Sometimes it's the reverberation of past times triggered by the scent of a passing woman, the melody of a near forgotten tune or the angle of the sun through a tree. These are the moments to be recognized and cherished. They are the rewards of time and experience and proof of our own subtle, yet indelible mark left on the world.

Happiness
Is freely given. It's a small gift bestowed. It's 2 young squirrels chasing each other around a tree trunk creating a swirling, grey barber-pole while you wait at the bus-stop. It's

the weight of your car with a full tank of gas. It's the glance you get from a lover when you're about to say something stupid. It's when the butter is the perfect consistency to spread on your English Muffin. It's freely given, yes, but it demands attention. It demands notice. It demands appreciation. It demands a brief amount of your time and acknowledgment in order to flower.

Happiness
Can be cultivated. Time is its vehicle. Perspective is its currency. It lives in the mundane like a daisy in a junkyard. The icy cold wind in your face while shoveling snow can be a cleansing joy or a damp misery. The crying of children in church can be an annoyance or the affirmation that an institution will continue through the generations. Reading the last page of an excellent book can be a dreaded loss or a cause for celebration. Cultivate your joy. Nurtured with warmth and understanding and patience, it will grow.

Happiness
If shared will flourish. Our personal joys provide a glimpse to the bedrock of our souls. Let your dog know just how fluffy and warm you find her ears to be. Her pleasure will be palpable. Tousle your kid's hair, even if they're 25 and asking you for money. Show your partner the thing in Facebook that made you laugh. Smell the last tattered rose in the garden and appreciate the petals of her siblings scattered across the ground.

Happiness
Is fleeting. Is enduring. Is available. Is rare. It is the mixed scents of ocean and funnel-cake. It is the night sky in an especially dark place. It is the unexpected phone call. It is the hot tea steaming up our reading glasses. It is comfort and trust. It is surprise and serendipity. It is a hand-written letter and a 4-word text message. It's the moment after a sneeze.

It's the moment before the elevator stops. It is personal. It is public. It is a cascade of leaves from an unexpected gust of October wind. It will fill you if you allow it. Let it be.

*June, 202**

Hiya my Charlie,

It's officially summertime. This foggy, humid morning will attest to that. Here's my topic of the day. Happiness.

As a general rule, Mc's, Mc*'s, the Irish, the Catholics, in fact all the American's living in the NE of the US, all tend to be an unhappy bunch. I believe that's true. Not due to a lack of anything. Not due to an oppressive situation. Not due to persecution, war, pestilence, famine or monsters.*

Our unhappiness is due to our brains. Our outlook, our perspective, our corresponding actions to remedy our outlook and perspective. Our perceived hurts, imagined wrongs, dire anticipated consequences of actions not even yet taken, anxiety over things that will never actually occur. All these things suck the life out of everyday existence for no good reason.

The elder statesmen of thought will tell us to live in the moment and let tomorrow take care of itself.

We know that's some bullshit. We know prior planning prevents poor performance. We know that productivity, owning many things, saving up enough dough to take a week off at a coastal amusement park means happiness and success. We know people are watching, weighing, scrutinizing and judging.

That's the rub. As members of the human race, members of families, members of society, members of companies, members of a neighborhood, we know people are paying attention. And we care. We don't want to fall short. We don't want to disappoint or lose what we've got or get beat by a lesser individual.

Well, that's some bullshit too. The fact is, most people are way too self-absorbed to give much of a shit about anything unless it affects their bottom line.

If I can give anything to you as a Dad, let it be the ability to be happy. You are a bear of large heart and large brain. You are good and strong and a smart citizen. That's all anybody sees. Nobody's vested enough in your personal story to throw your life off its tracks. If you receive criticism from any quarter, it's 95% their issue and 5% yours. You can't fall short of anything if you are happy and content in your heart.

So be content. Encourage what makes you whole. Enjoy something in each minute of the day. Cultivate the relationships that bring you smiles and peace. Worry less about what 'they' think and act with your focus on the good, the beneficial, the mellow, the happy according to Charlie.

Me and Mom's upbringing was all about rules, expectations, and punishment. Shut up and do your job. Offer up your suffering to God. Straighten up or go to hell. OBEY the infallible priest, teacher, bible, doctor, policeman or bear the consequences.

It's a tough indoctrination to escape but I hope we didn't ingrain it too deeply in you and your brudder.

Foster your own happiness regardless of the world swirling around you. The shit you see on the news today will be the same shit you see on the news 40 years from now. Trust me, I'm witnessing it. Stupidity abounds. Retards never sleep.

Any dumb thing a human being can possibly do has been done a million times before to the same exact result. You just need to find your philosophical space, optimize what makes you you and do your thing without unnecessary external influences.

The reality of what you are appreciating right now will always beat the scary shit your brain is attempting to foist on you. Enjoy and don't worry. It'll all be fine. 100 billion people who ran through their existence from beginning to end would tell you the same thing if they could.

Be good.
Love,
Dad

"Our so-called leaders speak
With words, they try to jail ya.
They subjugate the meek
But it's the rhetoric of failure."

Spirits In The Material World– The Police, Ghost in the Machine, 1981

Chapter 10
Life and Death

*Winter 201**

Hiya Mikey,

Hope you are doing well and are healthy and content and happy.

Pop's brother Uncle John died yesterday. He got a fast-moving brain tumor that wiped him out in 2 weeks. Not a bad way to go for an old-timer. He avoided laying around in a diaper fighting some extended battle with cancer or stroke damage. I won't expect you and Charlie to fly in for the funeral, but I am glad he came to your graduation party. He saw our house and bar and how awesome our kids are.

Anyway, here is some insight into perseverance. It's a necessary quality to meet goals. Some of it is genetic, some of it is learned behavior. I believe your mother and I have done well in business due to several factors, but one of the main ones is getting up every day and going to work. I believe it is an ingrained behavior, an Irish Catholic Working-Class behavior. We watched our parents get up every day and go to work. Every. Day. That was Uncle John. There was no boning, crying or expecting something for nothing. There was no sick time or handouts.

The old timers called people like this "Salt of the Earth". Most of America is like this. Most of America are middle of the road pragmatists. We're the ones who pay the taxes that the government uses to educate you, protect our country, build roads and support illegals and lazy shits who don't work. So yeah, 1/2 the battle of perseverance is just showing up.

The other part is attitude and competence. Whingers use complaints as an excuse. Moaners don't get the job done. Sad sacks piss everyone off and are disruptive to the job.

The strong-willed people fight through problems and circumstances and refuse to let bullshit get in the way of doing an excellent job. One thing I stress to hiring managers is this concept. "Do you want an employee who is awesome sometimes or good every day." I'd take the 'good every day' guy every time.

Perseverance takes backbone and a high tolerance for pain. These are 2 things you have in spades.

Here's some insight from people who understood the concept:

- *The path from dreams to success does exist. May you have the vision to find it, the courage to get on to it, and the perseverance to follow it. Kalpana Chawla*
- *Success is no accident. It is hard work, perseverance, learning, studying, sacrifice and most of all, love of what you are doing or learning to do. Pele*
- *Patience and perseverance have a magical effect before which difficulties disappear and obstacles vanish. John Quincy Adams*
- *Grit is that 'extra something' that separates the most successful people from the rest. It's the passion, perseverance, and stamina that we must channel in order to stick with our dreams until they become a reality. Travis Bradberry*
- *I do not think that there is any other quality so essential to success of any kind as the quality of perseverance. It overcomes almost everything, even nature. John D. Rockefeller*
- *Of all that is good, sublimity is supreme. Succeeding is the coming together of all that is beautiful.*

Furtherance is the agreement of all that is just. Perseverance is the foundation of all actions. Lao Tzu

- *If your determination is fixed, I do not counsel you to despair. Few things are impossible to diligence and skill. Great works are performed not by strength, but perseverance. Samuel Johnson*

Stay Strong.
Love,
Dad

*January, 202**

Hiya Mike,

You got new blinds yesterday. They look great. No wonky nonsense anymore. I also got the closet barn door kits delivered. That'll be my project for the weekend (in addition to taking down Xmas and the trees.....pfff). It's supposed to be rainy anyway.

So you're winding down your first week in your 4th semester. Good stuff. I hope it's been smooth and mellow for you.

I saw you ordered The Merchant of Venice. I was a Freshman in High School Lit Class with Mr. Kay when we read that book in the spring. Kay was a little guy with pink tinted reading glasses and a 70's mustache. He was funny as balls and brilliant...and gay as a 4-dollar bill. But that wasn't much of a big deal in mid-century Catholic schools. He had an apartment in town and lived with 4 cats. Me, Fred and Squat would stop by his house occasionally and hang out and break his balz. Great human being. He would go to NYC routinely for Broadway shows and hung the yellow and black playbills from all the shows he'd seen around his classroom. There were hundreds of them.

Anyway, he was a great teacher and very observant. I sat

in the middle row upfront, 1 or 2 desks in. Nina Arnoldo was a smoking hot, quiet little Italian girl with long brown hair and big brown eyes who sat in the 1st isle near the wall, 2 seats down.

Kay must've noticed that I had my eye on Nina. When he broke out the MofV, he assigned kids in the class to read the various roles. He gave me Bassanio, and he gave Nina the Portia character, Bassanio's love interest. It was a lot of fun and we got to know each other a little bit. Never dated or anything but were friends. I was shy as shit. Still am. I had plans on calling her up during the summer for a date but never did. I was running a printing press during the day and hanging around with the crew at night and the time just slipped away.

That summer, a brain tumor from out of nowhere killed Nina Arnoldo dead. I never got the chance to catch up with her and explore things. Kinda sucked. Some of her last words to me were from Shakespeare.

"But the full sum of me Is sum of something which, to term in gross, is an unlessoned girl, unschooled, unpracticed; Happy in this—she is not yet so old but she may learn. Happier than this— She is not bred so dull but she can learn. Happiest of all is that her gentle spirit Commits itself to yours."

Oofaa.

So, the lesson here is to act on situations right away if they present themselves. If you see something cool, grab it before it's gone (dinosaur fossil). If you see a person of interest, talk to them. If you are witnessing something that's totally boss. Witness it with full concentration and engagement and commit the sights, sounds, smells and feelings to memory.

Life's pleasures are made up of small moments, people and situations that live in your mind. People forget the bad shit, but the good stuff is forever. Look for the potential and make the effort to fold it into your life. You'll be a happier and more fulfilled and connected person for the effort. This is just another version of the Nike slogan. But true nonetheless.

Epilogue: They had a Fall Memorial at school for Nina with 5000 kids at Mass in the HS Auditorium. Mr Kay taught for many more years at the school with nary an issue with the 1000's of kids he taught while the priests and other teachers around him dropped like flies. He retired a few years ago and volunteers at the Town ASPCA taking care of the cats. One of the genuinely great teachers and genuinely good dudes.

And yeah, Shakespeare can still break your heart in multiple ways.

Stay Strong.
Love,
Dad

Here we need to take a quick breath and consider. Revisiting this gives me a weltschmerz for lost opportunity and stolen potential. In full disclosure, I never had the light-bulb moment of realizing Mr. Kay purposefully matched Nina and I in that exercise until I recounted the story in the letter to Mike above. I guess I regarded it as happenstance. Not only does it highlight the thickness of my Irish cranium, it also heightens my respect for Kay as a brilliant social engineer and creator of his own fun. He was giving a shy kid a shot. I waited too long.

Mr. Kay's since shuffled off this mortal coil but I remember him fondly and have molded some of his wry humor and penchant for written Easter Eggs into my own character. I notice the same humorous writing style in both my boys. Mr. Kay lives on.

A guy in the back wants to know about "(dinosaur fossil)" in the letter above.

Well Sir, let's use this opportunity to boister off the sads with an adventure. File this under the heading, "Grab it Before it's Gone."

Once upon a time we were travelling out west. It was likely summertime. It was somewhere near the New Mexico and Colorado border. My boys at the time were probably in late grade school, early high school. We all dug cowboys and had spent some epic time previously among the buffalo in the Black Hills and Badlands. We were out West once again, whistling down the way, looking for trouble in a desert border town.

One quick Western aside, inside a sidenote, if you'll indulge me. You've heard about our work/daycare/home commutes before. Here is the car soundtrack of those early years. It's a very short list.

- Jingle Jangle Jingle – Riders in the Sky

They liked Ghost Riders, Big Iron, Strawberry Roan, El Paso type stuff but Jingle Jangle was the favorite. Jingle Jangle was the requested de-escalator. On repeat. Being 2.40 minutes long, it took roughly between 10 and 17 repetitions to get home depending on traffic. Yipeeeaaaay! Both boys naturally took to Cowboy songs right from the start. I blame Elmo in a cowboy hat and Marty Robbins Album covers.

I have vivid memories of picking up a hot and sweaty Charlie from the daycare, stuffing him into a sizzling car seat. I'd start the car, crank up the AC and see how his day went.

More often than not, he would already have his emergency car binky firmly in place and mumble a very surly and menacing, "Bingle Bingle" at me, glaring through his bangs. Tough day.

We would ride in comfortable, air-conditioned silence nursing our daily grudges and mellowing out while Ranger Doug and his talented band of Cowboys sung about the glories of avoiding marriage.

Why? Boys. That's why. Make sure your insurance is paid up.

**"I got spurs that jingle, jangle, jingle
As I go ridin' merrily along
And they sing, "Oh, ain't you glad you're single"
And that song ain't so very far from wrong."**

Jingle Jangle Jingle - Riders in the Sky, Cowboy Songs, 1996

But this isn't about that. Our Cowboy predilection finds us on a dusty border road passing a home-made sign that reads "Rock Shop" with an arrow pointing down a dustier border road. The lovely and elusive Autumn my wife excitedly pointed and hooted so I General Lee'd a rooster tail onto Rock Shop Trail in our underpowered, rented SUV from National. GenX at its best.

A few miles down the trail, rising from the dun environment like a Tatooine Moisture Farm came series of low, white adobe and block buildings, scattered pieces of huge rusting mining assemblies and coal carts full of stone. We pulled into a gravel lot better paved than the roadway and parked next to an honest-to-shit tumbleweed. An ancient, sand-blasted slab of wood proclaiming "Rock Shop" creaked like a scary show on thick rusted chains. I told the lovely and elusive Autumn my wife, "If there's a Chinaman in there selling Gizmos, we're out." I turned to instruct the boys not to touch nuthin, 'specially gremlins, but they were already well into a game of tetanus roulette among the towering ramps and trommels 1/4 mile away.

The Rock Shop turned out to be a wonderland of geology, gemology, volcanology, archeology and whatever 'ology' does dinosaurs, meteors, and fossils. Enough to satisfy the curiosity of very curious boys and discerning spouses. The items for sale were distributed in bins, on shelves, walls, wheelbarrows, buckets and carts across several lots and several buildings. The staff was seasoned, knowledgeable and friendly.

The place rocked. The stuff was killer. Mike immediately quested for the biggest coprolite he could find. Look it up. Charlie was eyeing up a bison of carved onyx. The lovely and elusive Autumn my wife was choosing between two beautiful Navajo silver wrapped smooth stone pendants.

In the corner of one small adobe hut, hanging from a hank of twine on a 5-penny nail against an aquamarine painted plaster wall, was a thin slab of grey stone the size of a marble copybook. Swimming across this slab of stone was a perfect, full body, fossilized baby Loch Ness monster type dinosaur. Every rib, vertebra, fin, and tooth rippling in and out of the stone matrix. Unprecedented and way too cool. It had the technical dinosaur's name on a tag, but don't ask me. It was boss. It looked like the real. It was screaming to come home with us. The tag said $800.00. I said, "Hell, Naw." and I left it there.

The lovely and elusive Autumn, my wife secretly took the store's card with the intent to purchase the dinosaur fossil and have it shipped for my birthday or Christmas.

When she called, they could not remember or identify any fossil on site that matched that description. The fossil's spot in the aquamarine hut was now occupied by a fossilized slab of ferns. My swimming dinosaur was gone like it never existed. Opportunity blown. Lesson learned. On with life. It was probably effing haunted or something anyway.

*September, 202**

Hey There Mikey,

Txt said your Krimpets got there yesterday. Might take a bit to get to your box. They should be good and fresh hopefully.

I went to Joe Pipes funeral on Saturday. 87 years old. Had a stroke. Went to bed one night and woke up dead. Not a bad way to go. He was a great friend and a great male role model. Very smart, very funny and very dedicated to whatever he was involved with at the time. He was a Colonel in the Army. Afterwards, he got up at 0430, took a train to NYC, negotiated labor contracts between maritime unions and the companies that owned giant tankers and came home to teach people like me and Old Jim how to play the bagpipes at night. The female minister of his church said that he was mowing their lawn 2 weeks ago.

Let's talk about role models a minute. Guys need good male role models. I've always looked toward my older friends, family, co-workers and acquaintances for traits I admire and wanted to emulate or fold into my personal routine. It could be their style of humor, their way of accomplishing tasks, their way of interacting with others, their speech patterns, actions, dress, anything.

Pop's ability to fix anything, his way of calmly handling stress, his iron-willed work ethic are things I've tried to emulate with varying degrees of success. He's a brilliant, basic dude who just does not flex. Not to his wife, not to cancer, not to a broken car, not to sepsis, not to anything. He does his thing and nothing stops him.

My sisters got a lot of Pop in them, as do I, as do you. Want to know where your subversive sense of humor comes from? Next time you're home, ask Pop about that news show years ago where some Asian country was about to get nailed by a tsunami. He sat glued to the tv watching 100's of people run to the seaside boardwalk to watch the tidal wave come in. He was laughing so hard when they got washed away by a 65-foot wall of water that he almost pissed himself.

Needless to say, we were all laughing too but G'Mom was horrified.

We saw Old Jim on Saturday too. He's got one leg in the hole and his other leg's giving out, so be prepared. Jim was a good role model for different stuff altogether. He worked hard, had money and enjoyed using it to make a better life for himself and his family. His hunting trips, guns, bows, cars, trophies, even his donations to the church were all because he could. His money, his fun, his time. No guilt, no explanation. It takes a ballsy person to live a life like that. I'm sure he learned that from a male role model somewhere down the line.

So, pay attention to the people you are surrounded by. You never know when a word, a trait, a strut or an action will resonate with who you are and who you want to grow into. Be selective. I've probably shed 100 temporary skins over the years keeping what worked and dumping what didn't.

Everybody's got good in them but I want to fold the great into my core. You'll know you're doing it right when people start to emulate you. And believe me, that day is not far off.

Stay Strong.
Love,
Dad

*9/11/201**

Hiya Mike,

I just wrote your brother a letter. It's 9/11. You were but a wee sprat when Islamic extremists used fully fueled US aircraft to kill Americans. It was a devastating dose of reality for the country. There are people out there who want to hurt us because they believe that's what their God wants. It's very hard to fight a belief system.

I told your brother since he lives in a city, he needs to always keep his eyes open, always have an escape route and know exactly how and when to get himself out of harm's way.

Your situation is different. There are probably only a scant handful of places in the world as secure as where you are right now. That's a comfort to us. It is also nice to know you will be honing and utilizing your considerable talents to make the world a better and safer place. That should fill you with pride and fuel your daily efforts. I know it makes us proud. To Bury the Mike under a Bushel Basket would be a high crime.

"Neither do men light a candle, and put it under a bushel, but on a candlestick; and it giveth light unto all that are in the house. Let your light so shine before men, that they may see your good works." Matt. 5 Verses 14 to 16

I'd like to believe that was a big factor in your choosing the Academy. You've always believed in yourself. You could be destined for big things and writing fluff papers at Schmo U is probably not the appropriate venue to explore the possibilities and challenge your potential.

No matter how hard things get, remember that your choice was a great one. My boys have never taken the easy road. They work hard. They work smart, and they win.

Anyway, you have always known your job. Please try to enjoy the ride. Remember to laugh, make sure you have fun along the way. Get some sun, get some snow, get some joy from the small stuff. We love you.

Stay strong.
Love,
Dad

*March, 202**

Hi There my Charlie,

Nice to finally see some snow. It's been a soft, warm winter. Pfff. Good for heating costs, bad for playing outside and getting extra shoveling reps in. If the weather trend continues, you won't have to move south of Virginia if you want to retire in a warm climate when the time comes.

So, I wrote my friend Declan a physical letter for the first time in years. When he lost his oldest son 9 years ago, I sent

Declan writing paper, envelopes and a nice fountain pen. Why? Because writing letters is personal. Writing letters requires physical and mental concentration. Especially with dire topics, especially with a temperamental fountain pen. Writing letters requires thought and commitment.

We exchanged letters that year and months following. Our sons were the same age. There was a lot to process. Dec told me that letter writing gave him some respite from his grief and an outlet for his thoughts without judgment.

Consider making letters part of your deal. Short, written, Thank You notes are an extinct practice that will define you as a person of distinction and refinement. If a board member backs you up and says something nice, send him a quick written note of thanks. It will spread goodness and you will be remembered. If some intern slouch goes the extra mile to deliver an excellent result for you. Send them a quick Thank You email and copy the team. That will grease the way for the next person to step up their game. Positive reinforcement. Plus, you are leaving behind an artifact of The Charlie. Don't underestimate the value of an artifact.

Think of it this way. When the last person who knew me dies, I'm gone. All that's left are some artifacts. You'll have work papers galore. Leave some personal artifacts.

So, Declan's 2nd son is gone now too. We haven't heard how and it really doesn't matter. He was your age. Dec's lost 2 sons. Charlie, if I lost you or Mike, I'd be broken beyond fixing. If I lost you both, well, that's a hole I'd have trouble crawling out of.

I've given you the screed before but remember this; as sentient beings, we feel all of the good and bad in the world. Life is uncomfortable. Life is cold, wet, difficult, mean and unfair. Life is unfair to the flower that gets hit by a hailstorm, life is unfair to the ant that gets stepped on by an endangered Galapagos Tortoise, life is painful, unfeeling and undiscerning. Once you understand that, you are free to enjoy the juxtaposition. Mean lets you appreciate Nice. Cold lets you appreciate Warmth. Work lets you appreciate Play.

The Stoics will tell you to value time over money or things. After all, what's alive will one day not be. Focus on what you can control. Don't suffer from imagined troubles. Hold your emotions and impressions up to a bright light before you act on them. Learn something from everyone. Be a product of good habits and good thinking. Ditch whatever's non-essential in your life. Add whatever brings you peace of mind.

You've already proven to be one goddamned, bulletproof boss of a person. Brains, brawn, purpose and means. You've got tools most people would kill for. Do your Charlie thing. Improve your Charlie thing. Be a happy and productive Charlie.

We are all still here to assist and witness.

Be good.
Love,
Dad

"I thought you'd always be there, I almost believed you."

In Too Deep – Genesis, Invisible Touch, 1987

Chapter 11
Father's Day

*June, 201**

Hiya my Charlie,

Finally, it's June. June always harkened the end of school and my birfday and nice weather. When you were born, June added Father's Day for me. No one comes into being a Dad with any script or rule-book. The whole pregnancy thing is a 9-month spring training camp of crazed hormones, "What to Expect" books, doctor's appointments, parental advice which is hopelessly outdated, loss of sleep and gradual acceptance that your life is never going to be the same. Once the birth actually happens, it'll be kind of a relief. You'll be used to lack of sleep, appointments and spousal craziness. Even though you're not there yet. It'll be good to remember.

Now, I can't speak for others, but prior to parenthood, I viewed other people's kids and babies as somebody else's problem at best and totally annoying and gross at worst. I'm content not to be the 'fun uncle'. When I had my own little boy, nothing really changed except I now had a little buddy to whom I could explain why everybody else's kids are annoying and gross. It was totally awesome. Having a little guy to play with, show stuff, buy cool toys for and the million other things we got to do in those early years was a ton of fun.

We tend not to remember the toxic shits, stomach bugs, temper tantrums and not so pleasant things with as sharp a clarity as the good stuff. That's also because there are so many more good times than bad. We were lucky that way. You were a great kid, sharp, funny, strong, observant, resilient, pleasant. Being introduced into parenthood by a baby like you was like winning a giant lottery. You were the defining force behind some of my best lifelong memories. Playing blocks in the chair, creating the Ninja Finger game, putting together 1200-piece toys, bikes and stuff at midnight on Christmas Eve. I bet you wish you still had that awesome giant chopper bike from 100 years ago.

The next big thing for a Dad is letting your baby out into the wild. It seems like school starts immediately after you don't need diapers anymore. You were only just a very wee Charlie when you started Kindergarten. It was a gut punch watching you get on a bus or watching the school door close behind you and wondering how it's gonna go. That, at least for me, has never changed. Leaving you anywhere, even as a 20 something college student, was just as hard as watching your little red shirt and backpack walk into the old school. You nailed that whole thing with the skill of a total boss from day one. We shouldn't have worried, but that's what parents do.

So, thank you for introducing me into the concept of Fatherhood. I'm happy and proud of the results. Parenting is never about the parents. It's about the child. Teaching is never about the teacher. It's about the student. You were very lucky to have young, enthusiastic, and kind teachers. Your success is their success as well as our success. But the big win is you. Always will be.

Mike doesn't get an email like this one simply due to timing. If fatherhood was a baseball mitt, mine was new and fresh and hard to break in. It took years of oiling, getting slammed with fast-balls and scraping for grounders before it was broken in and serviceable. You took the brunt of new fatherhood and did remarkably well despite my dropped fly balls, pickles and rain delays. By the time your brudder rolled around, my fatherhood mitt was well-oiled and fully functional. Sure, it had dents, nicks, scrapes and stains, but it was broken in and knew the job. This was a good thing because Mike took more work.

Anyway, your success was always more you than anyone else. As far as sons go, I wouldn't change a goddamn thing about you or your brudder. You are the sons other people dream of having and I appreciate that. And I appreciate you.

Your arrival gave Mom and I a purpose outside ourselves and it has been an excellent adventure.
I'm gonna have a good Father's Day and it's due to you my Charlie. Thank you.

Be good.
Love,
Dad

Now, I feel the need to level-set just a bit. Simply so Good-Time Cholly above doesn't get a big head. Yeah, his birth was not fun as you'll find out and he was cool and all but.

In the 90's, the baby doctor tending to the lovely and elusive Autumn my wife, recommended she drink 1 Guiness Nitro Pounder a day while she was nursing. Why? GenX Doctors. That's why. He prescribed me 4.

The narrow, 10lb meat-tube that she delivered at the hospital, the one with a screaming hole at both ends? Well, in a few weeks' time he turned into a hippopotamus. Bristly on top, otherwise bald, greazy, hangry, a couple giant teeth. Then he got too fat to move. I blame and salute Arthur Guiness.

We had to create methods to encourage him to ripple across the floor like a miniature sea elephant. Grandmom would scootch behind him tickling his feet. The lovely and elusive Autumn my wife would encourage him with a favorite toy.

Me? I would put peanut butter on his feet and we'd both laugh while the cat chased him around the room. Why? Denis Leary will tell you at the end of the next chapter.

*January, 202**

Hiya my Charlie

Today, on National Irish Coffee Day, while you're heading to parts unknown for work, during a questionable winter storm, take a moment to see yourself, 5, 10, 15 years out from today. What's the same, what's different? You've nailed your 25-year plan. Now's the time to quietly ponder your next orders of business. What gets priority, what gets shelved, what gets considered, what gets rejected.

Security gives you the time and freedom to plan while other folks sweat to make the rent with no thought to the future. Just something to consider.

So, the doogan's been doing this thing where she wakes us up at 230am and makes us take her up the street for a dump at the field. She got me Monday morning and Mom yesterday. We'll have to put a hard stop on this nonsense. We're modifying her food intake to no people food or meals at night. We're gonna add a post-dinner walk to hopefully tire her out more as well. Mom thinks she's getting senile because that's what old folks do. I don't think she's getting senile. She's just turning into a demanding old lady like they'll tend to do.

I was thinking the other night, after Mom gave me my mid-winter back-skritch, that my hope is that you and your brother eventually find a nice woman to make a life with. Everybody needs a nice back-skritch from time to time. Why? Because you can't reach every spot that needs attention by yourself. Both you boyos will make outstanding husbands because you are smart, kind, motivated and extraordinarily well-gened.

You'd both be great fathers too. Why? Because you are funny, playful, caring, and protective.

Kids need care and protection, but mostly they need fun, play and the opportunity to do stuff on their own but under a watchful eye. No matter how big you get, how important you become, how lucrative your job is, the things that make life meaningful are never centered on you but on others.

I've placed literally a thousand people in new, big-money positions in my career and what I remember is Mom, in her teens, listening to tunes in my '75 Maverick, a little Mikey holding up the Math and Science Awards in grade school, You nailing a 25 foot downhill putt in front of the whole golf team.

The best rewards in my life have been small moments experienced by people I love.

In the big picture, stuff is nice but usually not appreciated or even remembered after the purchase. Friendships come and go and morph with time. When it comes to girls, I like Mark Twain's concept. "Those that go searching for love, only manifest their own lovelessness. And the loveless never find love, only the loving find love. And they never have to seek for it."

The way I read the above quote is "Become the person you would look for in a partner and the right person will find you." There's no clock ticking, there's no expectations, just live your best life and let stuff unfold.

So, here's to a safe and mellow trip to the Apple. Grab some street food if you can. The roasted chestnut guys should be out. Don't eat 'em, just put the hot bag in your pocket to warm your hands.

Be good.
Love,
Dad

"A lovestruck Romeo sang the streets a serenade
Laying everybody low with a love song that he made
Finds a streetlight, steps out of the shade
Says something like, "You and me, babe, how about it?"

Romeo and Juliet - Dire Straits, Making Movies, 1980

*Oct, 201**

Happy Day Before Your Birthday Cholly!

You had a long and difficult birth. Started Friday around 4am and you finally appeared around 6pm on Sunday. You were a big, long baby and comfortable where you were over a week past your due date. It took a lot of urging to get you interested in daylight. When you finally busted out, and you did bust out, it took a team of 2 doctors and 2 nurses to put Mom back together.

My intro into fatherhood was holding you, all wrapped up in a blanket, for the first 1 hour of your existence, while Mom got worked on. You were quiet and I talked to you. You definitely recognized my voice. It must've sounded loud and un-muffled compared to what you were used to, but you were calm and very interested in the sights and the sounds. The next day, they sent us all home and we were on our own. Parenthood is a game with no manual but we worked together and separately to create love and security and opportunities for you.

We couldn't be prouder of who you are. Life is just a carnival ride of ups and downs but our inherent core of hard work, respect and brains never swerved off the path and never let us down. You've already learned that lesson through osmosis.

I miss the days where you would just snuggle up and lay on me while we watched some tube but little guys never stay little. Having kids is signing up for the full trip. The ride continues to be epic. Thank you for making me a Dad. It's the title I'm most proud to have.

Here's some rules for a good life from the Cowboys. Consider as you carve another notch on your pistol grip:

- *Every trail has some puddles.*
- *There's no place 'round the campfire for a quitter's blanket.*

- *Tossin' your rope before buildin' a loop don't ketch the calf.*
- *Polishing your pants on saddle leather don't make you a rider.*
- *A closed mouth gathers no boots.*
- *Don't name a cow you plan to eat.*
- *Never miss a good chance to shut up.*
- *Life is not about how fast you run, or how high you climb, but how well you bounce.*
- *Keep skunks, lawyers, and bankers at a distance.*
- *Life is simpler when you plough around the stump.*
- *If you find yourself in a hole, the first thing to do is stop diggin'.*
- *Don't sell your mule to buy a plough.*
- *Never corner something meaner than you.*

Be good.
Love,
Dad

Now before the pro-choice/pro-life screamers get riled up. My use of the word 'existence' in the letter above has zero deeper meaning beyond the fact that I was now holding my new son. Your arguments about the semantics and timing of 'life' are your own and I don't care.

The lovely and elusive Autumn my wife was recently involved in a corporate team building exercise. The moderator went around the room asking each person to describe an accomplishment. Drivel about projects and deadlines and work stuff was proposed until they got around to my wife. She stood up and proclaimed that her biggest accomplishment was delivering not 1 but 2, 10-pound baby boys with zero medication or painkillers. Even though it wasn't a competition, she sat down with the win. Why? GenX women. Don't expect nonsense.

Now, I just happened to be in the room while these births

took place, so I know the immensity of her ordeal and why this feat, most effectively, obscured 30 plus years of cutting-edge scientific research, double digit publications and patents to be dominating her personal Rushmore. Why? Miracles and such notwithstanding, childbirth is a dirty, nasty, hurtful bitch. We were both totally pro drugs too. In both instances, the lovely and elusive Autumn my wife had progressed beyond the safe administration of epidurals and whatever else could have eased the exit. Damn overachiever. It was bad when it happened the first time. I have scars from her embedded fingernails to prove it. You know the rest.

Then it happened again on round 2. My wife was told she could not be safely given pain medication. She sat up in bed like Nos-friggin-feratu and bellowed such a rolling litany of nuclear-grade, uncensored invective that Black Philip busted out of a closet and ran down the hall, hooves sparking in terror. The doctor who delivered the news just saw a big flash and woke up on a Dr's Without Borders Bus in Honduras.

What came out of my wife that day was awesome, impressive, scary and eye opening and I'm talking about both ends. It crystalized in me a very deep respect for what she and the human body is capable of withstanding. It also prompted me to purchase a shotgun "for the house" without telling her. Why? GenX Females. That's why. Back away slowly and don't show fear.

So, at the end of the story, the lovely and elusive Autumn my wife is the founder of my Father's Day. She dealt. She dealt like a bloodied and pissed off shield maiden with a sharp spear and horrendous vocabulary. She delivered my new, beautiful baby boy to complete the set and we all won.

Me? I just held her hand, manned the bucket and hoped I'd be able to catch up someday.

"A word in your ear, from father to son
Hear the word that I say
I fought with you, fought on your side
Long before you were born."

Father to Son – Queen, Queen II, 1974

Chapter 12
Recipes

Recipes, you ask. Yeah, recipes. You'll see in the letters below that my personal theory of male adulthood includes the ability to feed yourself and others with understated skill and execution. Why? Because boys eat. They eat a bunch, and they eat often. They also eat much smarter these days than we did. If they can whip up a meal that's cheaper, healthier, and tastier than your average McDoink's shit-burger, they will do it. They just need to see that it is possible and pretty easy to accomplish. Plus, and this is a big plus, girls dig a guy who can cook.

I came by my cooking chops by a mixture of love and necessity. My Mom was an effortless chef in the kitchen. She could coalesce a pepper, egg and cheese sammy on a hoagie roll on demand out of thin air. She could present a crown roast and all the trimmings for a Christmas feast, singing a song, with nary a smudge on her apron. I never realized what a skill this was until I did it myself. Gordon Ramsey my ass. No screaming was ever necessary in the kitchen.

From the other side of the spectrum, my Dad sometimes sliced a banana onto his bowl of Special K if he was feeling fancy. The first time he was responsible for feeding us, we learned the social etiquette of eating at the counter of the local hoagie shop. Namely, "Don't spin your sibling off the stool." When he finally witnessed us making actual meals in grade school, he was totally off the hook.

As GenX kids, we witnessed the last of the Flintstones Era where Dads were the providers while Moms were the nourishers. More and more frequently, both parties worked and we, the kids, were on our own for food. That particular train just gained speed and kids who didn't learn how to provide for themselves were either broke or just plain hungry.

My boys witnessed the lovely and elusive Autumn my wife plan and prepare meals. My boys witnessed their old man plan and prepare meals. Hell, I'm personally responsible for a very conservative 4000 hand-made, hand-packed lunches they scarfed throughout their school careers. When they were out on their own, they needed to plan and prepare meals too. Done right, it's smart, healthy and economical. It's always felt like a privilege for me to feed my family and I miss the big noisy meals. GenX cooks. Why? We're practical and we have taste.

The recipes in the letters below are simple, or guidelines, or just tasty booze concoctions so I'll start you off with a real, live, personal recipe. This is my chili recipe that won First Place *and* the People's Choice award at our local Chili Cookoff.

If that doesn't make this chapter legit, nothing will.

Dad's East Texas Style Whole Steak Chili

Ingredients
- **1 big white onion chopped fine**
- **5 cloves garlic chopped fine**
- **4 serrano peppers scorched over an open flame and chopped fine**
- **4 jalapeno peppers scorched over an open flame and chopped fine**
- **1 yellow bell pepper chopped fine**
- **1 red bell pepper chopped fine**
- **1 orange bell pepper chopped fine**
- **3 lbs stew beef chunks chopped smaller**
- **1 can tomato paste**
- **1 big can crushed tomatoes**
- **1 big can chopped tomatoes drained**
- **Carton or 2 of beef broth**

- Salt
- Pepper
- 1 McCormick's chili packet
- 1 McCormick's hot southwestern chili packet
- Adobo powder
- Chipotle pepper powder
- Smoked paprika
- Liquid smoke

To Do
- Close bedroom doors and open a window.
- Heat up a heavy soup pot or dutch oven w/oil and sear meat garlic and onions w/saltnpeppa
- Dump in both chili packets and coat the stuff
- Cook for a few minutes till juicy
- Add chopped stuff
- Add 3 tomato products
- Stir up good, bring to a boil, judge consistency add beef broth if necessary.
- Cut heat to 1/2, cover and simmer for 2 hrs. o
- If you're the type who just MUST have beans in your chili. Now's the time.
- Add adobo/chipotle and a few dashes of liquid smoke during simmer to taste
- Check if more salt or pepper needed.
- Booyah

Optional
- Take off heat, let refrigerate overnight.
- On serving day leave 1 hour to finish
- Reheat slowly to boiling.
- Check taste for more chipotle and smoke
- Check for good consistency, add beef broth or boil off extra liquid.

To Serve

- Serve in a deep bowl with a chunk of crusty bread, maybe some shredded cheddar, sour cream or chopped scunnions on top if you're feeling fancy.

*September, 201**

Hiya Charlie,

Happy Tuesday. It's the day you can buy some stuff at the corner market and make a nice dinner since your classes end early this semester.

Here's a simple stir-fry recipe:

- *Chop up (into bite size) a pepper, a garlic clove (or powder), some onion, maybe broccoli or carrot or whatever fresh veg the guy has.*
- *Heat up wok on medium/high flame with a couple spoon-fulls of olive oil.*
- *Stir in veggies, shake on some soy sauce, garlic powder.*
- *Cook for about 5-8 minutes until they are as soft or crunchy as you want them.*
- *Dump onto a plate or bowl.*
- *Heat up wok again add oil.*
- *Stir in chopped (bite sized) chicken breast, or cleaned shrimp or sausage or beef strips or whatever protein the guy has.*
- *Cook until meat is not pink inside (or shrimp is pink). About 3-5 minutes.*
- *Throw veggies back into wok with the meat. Add a couple shakes of soy sauce or teriyaki.*
- *Heat up and serve on a dish or over rice or over egg noodles or in a pita or hoagie roll.*
- *Clean and put away your shit. They'll never know you were there, but they'll smell something awesome.*

Let me know how it goes!

By the way, it's 9/11 again. You're living in a city. Now is a good time to remember that there are religiously whacked-out shit-birds in the world who want to hurt you. Some of them are certainly downtown. Keep your eyes open. Always have a plan and an escape route. If shit goes really bad, really fast, move, keep moving and don't stop moving till you are well out of harm's way.

Be safe.
Love,
Dad

*November 201**

Hiya Charlie,

It's November, my 2nd favorite month next to October. But October was so stinking warm that it might lose its ranking. Of course, it's 70 degrees and raining right now. Gross. It looks like you will have a grey, wet Saturday but a sunny and cool Sunday.

On Wed night I wheeled the fire box onto the driveway, we set up a table with candy, got some chairs out and relaxed for Halloween. I made a big pitcher of my October Nor'easters. Excellent drink, but an expensive drink. Tito's vodka, Crown Royal Vanilla and Ginger Snap moonshine.

<u>*The October Nor'easter*</u>
- *Rocks glass filled with cubes.*
- *1.5 shots each:*
  - *Tito's*
  - *Crown Vanilla*
  - *Moonshine, (gingersnap, cinnamon, or apple moonshine)*

Top off with fresh cold apple cider and stir.

Moose came over with his wine, Aneet, Ben, your pal Frank all came over at various times and hung out. Got over 100 kids. I had full sized bars buried under a bunch of fun-sized shit, if kids were polite and put some effort into the costume, I would tell them to dig a little to get to the good stuff.

Mom said a fidget in a cowboy outfit came by. She said didn't know if he was 6, 16 or 60. I totally missed him. That would've made my night.

So you have less than 2 months before your semester is in the books. Home stretch my man. Unbelievable. Push hard rounding third.

I'm looking forward to seeing you on Thanksgiving. Your brother will love to hang with you. He hasn't been home since June. You'll both probably want to sleep for a full day in your own beds. With a doogan.

They closed the pool up 2 days ago. Now it looks like winter again. Oh well.

Have a good weekend. Be safe. Get your work done.

Love,
Dad

*July, 202**

Hiya my Charlie,

Here's the camping edition. There are a few basic facts of camping:

You're at the mercy of the weather. Hot sucks. Cold sucks. Rain sucks. Bugs suck.

Look at the nighttime temps at the location you'll be staying. You might end up sleeping on top of your bag if it's hot. If the bottom of your tent isn't advertised as totally waterproof, be careful where you plant it. No gullies, dips, washes or squishy ground.

Use a sleeping pad under your bag. Nothing like a pebble,

root, ants, or wet to ruin a night's sleep.

Bring a small knife and a larger knife or hatchet. For food, tinder, branches, logs, protection. Tip: Buy firewood along the way and save assache. Have firestarters or fat-stix or lighter fluid and a loaded zippo and matches.

Trash bags and foil and duct-tape are a camper's friend. Bring all 3.

Bring DEET bug stuff. A spray is easier to deal with. Plus, you can spray your tent screens with it. Bugs will ruin a trip if you're unprepared. If it's black-fly season in Maine, consider a head-net.

If you have room, bring a chair. Comfort makes a good time even better.

Food. If you're cooking on a fire a big, old cast iron skillet or grate is the best. If not, Veggies, spuds, salt, pepper, butter chopped and balled up in a foil packet and thrown in the fire are awesome. If you don't have a pan to sit on the fire, hot dogs on a green stick, burgers or steaks on a thin, flat piece of shale or flagstone will work. Make sure the rock's dry so it doesn't explode. Grease it with butter. Big knife or a stick to move the food. Hit a farm market along the way.

Breakfast. Pan with a little butter on the fire, cook your bacon and then scramble a pile of eggs in the grease. Toast some tortillas on a rock. Bacon grease will blow up, be careful. Use extra grease to coat some fire sticks if you're not in bear country.

If you are in bear country. Bring rope (bring rope anyway). Store your food in sturdy bag and hang from a tree branch at least 10 feet high. Don't cook near where you are sleeping. Cut yourself a solid 5 - 6 foot staff and sharpen the tip. Just in case. Keep it near. Helps with hiking too.

Nothing is better than campfire coffee at sunrise. Nothing worse than a hung-over hot, humid morning. Plan accordingly.

Playing cards. Ass-wipes. Extra clean water. Charged,

portable phone charger. Hat. Rag/bandana. Headlamp and batteries. Bathing suit, towel. Good bottle of whiskey or rum. Vodka doesn't camp. Sunscreen.

Have a 'No phone' rule.

Have your AAA card for road assistance. You break. You call. They come. Do not forget this tip.

Say yes to skinny dipping if you find a likely spot where you won't get arrested. Good place to clean up too.

Learn the night sky photo function on your phone. You may be able to take some epic shots.

Silence around a late night camp-fire is just a good as chatter. Enjoy the nature sounds. Might hear coyotes.

Anyway, that's what I got. Have a blast. Make sure everyone chips in for gas it'll be around $300 bucks round trip.

Be good.
Love,
Dad

*February, 202**

Hiya my Mikey,

Happy Friday! Time to do something nice for yourself. It's been 60 degrees and windy for most of the week here. Today is sunny and going up to a lusty 40 degrees but the wind is howling. I'll be cutting back the big grass and red-twig dogwoods at the top of the driveway today. Probably the Crepe Myrtle on the side too. It'd be nice to have an extra pair of hands but you're in the UK and Leo's hands are too small to be useful. Nobody's seen Frank for months. Mom's on the phone. Doogan's sitting in the dark bedroom wondering why everybody's up when it's so damn windy.

I made a Jambalaya yesterday. couple pounds of andouille sausage, giant swimps, veggies, rice and assorted goodies. Epic. We toasted some naan on the fire and feasted with

Chadds Ford sparkling apple cider. Packed up a couple containers for the P's. Although way too spicy for Grammy.

CRACKPOT JAMBALAYA

INGREDIENTS
- Vegetable oil cooking spray
- 2 cups onion, chopped
- 2 tablespoons minced garlic
- 1 cup celery, chopped
- 1 cup green pepper, chopped
- 1 bay leaf
- 15 ounce canned tomatoes
- 1/2 cup minced Italian parsley
- 5 pounds skinless chicken thighs
- 1 pound hot smoked sausage--sliced lengthwise, then across in semi circles
- 1 pound Andouille sausage--sliced lengthwise, then across in semicircles
- 1 pound raw peeled and cleaned swimps bigger the better
- 1/2 cup water
- Salt and pepper, to taste
- Hot Sauce and Cajun seasoning, habanero salt and smoked paprika to taste.
- 14 ounces long-grain rice (about 2-1/4 cups)
- 1 tablespoon minced fresh thyme
- 1 teaspoon Kosher salt

INSTRUCTIONS
- Use a large crockpot. Coat with vegetable spray.
- Mix vegetables and seasonings with canned tomatoes. Spread over bottom of crockpot. Tuck thighs into vegetable mixture. Top with chopped sausages. Pour water over, cover and cook on high for 4 hours.
- Remove cover and stir in rice, thyme and salt. Cover

and cook for an additional 50 minutes adding shrimp for the last 15 minutes of the 50. (Or until shrimp and rice are done).

- Alternatively, rice may be precooked separately and added near the end until heated through.
- Serve with bread of choice.

Enzo Palludi is coming on the 6th to get rid of the fallen willow and the dead ash up front. It's a shame to see the willow go. It was a pleasant tree to watch. I won't be missing the torpedo shaped leaves in the pool all summer long, however.

So, your big brudder is expecting to be forwarded as the next member of the Old School, School Board. The boy went out and chased it down on his own! A couple interviews and they'll vote him in in a week or 2. That's some great stuff. He says he'll be giving old Jim Bunn a raise in pay. 😄

Anyway, I hope you are making time for classes and making headway in your work and making food and fun a daily part of your UK adventure. Clock is ticking down very quickly, so be sure to hit the various sights and people and things you'd like to do while you're there. You could be stationed in a mid-western sand-pit with nothing but a Sonic within 60 miles. Instead, you're in a relatively compact center of global history with decent public trans. Good deal.

So enjoy the end of Winter and beginning of Spring. It might be warmer and less damp in a bit. Keep us informed about what's happening!

Stay Strong.
Love,
Dad

Then one day, out of the blue, Mike sent us a picture of his dinner. Penne in marinara with 4 huge meatballs, a spinach salad and garlic bread, giant beaker of ice water in the place where a wine might sit. Classic Mike feedbag. Made me proud. He was listening.

*August 202**

Hey There Mike,

That picture of your dinner was the best thing I've seen in a while! Beautiful and balanced. Great work!

Cooking is often a bypassed talent.

Everyone was pretty much expected to know how to make a few meals back in the day, but now, most people don't. Especially males. Males get a pass on cooking by the world in general, however, the alpha male knows how to cook.

The boners of the world need someone to make their own coffee. The me's of the world can feed an Ultimate Frisbee Team or whip up an intimate dinner for a cute girl, or a surf & turf for family Christmas with zero sweat, fuss or help. It's just another step in the quest for self-reliance, personal enrichment and being an effortlessly cool individual.

Here's my advice on cooking. Pick yourself 3 dinners to master. Master them according to the recipe. Then, master them using your own personal tweaks and touches. You have done this with breakfast, so you're already on your way. Make sure the dinners can be cooked on a regular gas/electric stove. You know you'll always have access to a cooktop.

Do the same for a couple sandwiches. BLT's are the easiest but tastiest and most impressive. Grilled cheese is up there too. Sausage and peppers on a roll, peppers and eggs on a roll. There's a million combos. Find a couple that speak to you. Make 'em. Eat 'em.

Desserts are easy. If you're having people over for dinner, have them bring dessert. Have some store-bought cookie dough on hand. The smell of fresh cookies makes a priceless impression.

A very easy and awesome dessert is a pre-made oreo pie crust from the store. You get a .99 cent instant chocolate pudding box, a tub of Cool Whip. Make the pudding (whisk with milk in a bowl, sit 5 minutes, done), carefully fold in 1/2 the cool whip into the pudding, spoon into the crust, blob some decorative cool whip on top and throw it in the freezer. Easy and awesome.

Just a thought. If you're making some cookies at home, like you do here sometimes, make a few more for the house. Put them on a plate in the kitchen with a note (Happy Tuesday!, Help Yourself!, For your coffee!). Simple, easy, good will. The hallmark of an effortlessly cool individual.

Anyway, that's my bit on cooking. You should know how to do. It's the skill that keeps on giving. It marks a person as erudite and accomplished.

And chicks totally dig a dude that can quietly and competently whip up a good meal. It's a stereotype buster. Glad you are well on your way to cook status. It's pretty easy and an awesome tool in your bag of skills.

Happy August. Hot and hoomid here. Pfff.

Stay Strong.
Love,
Dad

Before I wrap up this session on recipes, allow me another brief side trip. GenX tends to know where the party is. Fact is, the party is usually at their place. Our formative years witnessed brass cocktail shakers, 3 lb crystal cigarette lighters and roll-up bar-carts in real, non-ironic settings from generations who absolutely knew how to party. We absorbed much and continued the lessons.

It's frankly amazing to see all this stuff come back around to the younger, hipper folks. The difference for us is a matter of timing. In those days a person could make a living tending bar. The black-vested pros who tended bar when our parents took us to a real restaurant back in the day were capable of far more than just a Manhattan or Shirley Temple. They could easily slap you off the stool and carry you outside by your belt and collar for a quick lesson in civility, manners or holding your liquor. We've all seen it done. Why? 9 times out of 10 he was a veteran or owned the place. Usually both. Regardless, respect was expected, and a night out was special and treated as such.

Today's hipster tap-pullers in a 9-month-old brewery are like a Wacky-packages version of the real deal. I feel for those today who are searching for an experienced and accomplished adult to emulate and instead are forced to create a cartoon version of who they'd like to be simply because everyone around them is lame.

For those of you willing to take a page from qualified tipplers, I will leave this final recipe behind. Like my Chili above, it's a personal concoction.

I call it The Mayan Express. This recipe made its debut as my signature party drink in the early 2000's and has grown to be a staple in our neighborhood summertime Rum n Ribs gatherings, work events and important observances like the first Thursday of the Week. It's very, very deceptive in the tasty/potent ratio. Very smooth, delicious and packs a wallop. It has been known to clothesline experienced professionals. Its fame spread and the volume of stories and songs launched by The Mayan Express continues to grow. Why? To quote one of the high priests of GenX Comedy:

"You know, we spend a lot of time talking about death and disease and cancer and catastrophe and we do it because, well... I think it's fucking funny."

The Downtrodden Song - Denis Leary, No Cure for Cancer, 1992

Some folks never were exposed to The Rules of Drinking or learned to read instructions. And it shows. When The Mayan Express roars out of the depot with a brand-new passenger, I'm on the platform waving my hanky, laughing.

Why? Well, for the same reason I peanut-buttered the

baby's feet. I think it's fucking funny.

This recipe is made in a large glass iced tea/lemonade party jar that has a lid and a lower button-spout to dispense. It comes with a home-printed warning label taped to the lid and a full-color picture of a Dia De Los Muertos Sugar Skull taped on the jar. It says: **SERVE OVER A FULL CUP OF ICE. SIP.**

The Mayan Express

1 bottle white rum
1 bottle amber rum
1 bottle dark rum
1 bottle coconut rum
½ bottle 151 rum (that's the kicker)
1 small bottle Pom Juice
1 quart pineapple juice
2 mugs sweet black tea

Pour into jar, mix, add some sliced citrus or pineapple chunks if you can safely manage a knife.

Serve over a full cup of ice.

Let the party begin.

"So come fill up your glasses
Of brandy and wine
Whatever it costs I will pay
So be easy and free
When you're drinking with me
I'm a man you don't meet every day."

I'm a Man You Don't Meet Every Day– The Pogues, Rum Sodomy and the Lash, 1980

Chapter 13
Things to Remember Up to this Point

I know we've covered a lot of territory in the previous chapters. Here's a handy, dandy cheat-sheet of things to remember. The Cliffs Notes if you will. Just in case there's a quiz at the end.

Be glad I didn't make it a Mad Libs.

- **Don't look at the big flash.**
- **Keep the shitter clean.**
- **GenX females know the limitations of the male species like they issued a handbook.**
- **Happiness is a choice. It makes life nice.**
- **If it's working, don't mess with it.**
- **We tend not to remember the toxic shits.**
- **Boys. That's why.**
- **Nobody pays big bucks to a clown.**
- **We know that's some bullshit.**
- **Stupidity abounds.**
- **She misses you too.**
- **Comfort makes a good time even better.**
- **Vodka doesn't camp.**
- **People are way too self-absorbed to give much of a shit.**
- **Stay tight.**
- **What's real fun without some risk.**
- **Make a landing pad.**
- **A familiar comfort during a not so pleasant time.**
- **They put beans on the table.**
- **You are too valuable for that bush-league bullshit.**

- You haven't peaked, not by a long shot.
- The alpha male knows how to cook.
- Behold the Rules.
- We're nothing if not practical.

"This is our life, this is our song
We'll fight the powers that be, just
Don't pick on our destiny, 'cause
You don't know us, you don't belong."

We're Not Gonna Take It – Twisted Sister, Stay Hungry, 1984

Chapter 14
Death and Life

*9/11/202**

Hiya Mikey,

Happy September! It's the beginning of the best time of year. I am glad your time is ticking down in the UK. I gotta believe it was a fun adventure for a while but living abroad has to grate after an extended period. So get in, get presented, get done, get packed, get out. Lack of AC would just about make me bonkers. Just wait till you're in a US city with all the food and doings you were used to plus transportation and people to do stuff with.

Good luck on your physical tests today or tomorrow. You'd never enter a test without being prepared. Good work! When you're at the base, see if anyone has any info or connections where you're heading.

Today is 9/11. That day in 2001 started as just another workday. You and Charlie were at the daycare on Raglan Road near Mom's work. I was in a conference room at Digby Consulting. We were waiting for the meeting to begin when someone popped in at 8:45 and told us a plane had flown into the WTC. Initial reports said it was a small plane and likely pilot error or medical incapacitation. Then at 9am a second plane flies into Tower 2. That's when shit started to spin out of control. The Pentagon gets hit a 1/2 hour later. The plane crashes in PA 1/2 hour after that.

The worst was the people jumping from the towers. These were folks just like us who showed up for work. Now they were faced with a choice of burning or jumping. That's when the boss told us all to pack our shit and head home. Mom had already gotten you guys out of school and we all got home and sat in front of the news for what seemed like days. The pictures coming out of NYC were god-awful. The collapsing towers, the fleeing citizens, the dust, debris and rescue workers scrambling...

There's always a first time for everything, and this was the first time since Pearl Harbor that organized violence against US citizens was perpetrated on our soil. The first time that a foreign militant religious group had the audacity to target the US at home. It was the first time for many Americans to realize our insular group and home base was not as secure as all thought. Our freedom allowed skunks to enter our homes and plot our demise and execute a terminal plan. We lost people we knew personally when the towers came down. We had been in those towers ourselves many times. Now radical shit-birds blew huge holes into our infrastructure and things were about to change.

The number one thing I remember from those days is people being extremely pissed. The balls of these assholes using US flight schools to learn how to pilot fuel-loaded jumbo jets with the intention of using them like giant Molotov cocktails thrown at 500 miles an hour. Yeah, we were pissed. We were pissed as a whole. We were talking about turning entire countries into glass parking lots to send a message. And you know what? I was fine with that. If we had found out the exact locations where each of these terrorists had come from and systematically dropped a tactical nuke on those particular cities, I would have been happy. Number one. Fuck them. Number two. Fuck who harbored and trained them in terrorism. Number three. Fuck them again. You blow up a US building, on US soil, with US workers making a living, we'll disintegrate one of your zip codes and accept all the humanity and backlash that would entail. Then we'd do it again. Then we'd do it again. 4 planes,

4 repercussions. You wanna be a tough guy radical and take out the infidels and die a hero martyr, you best be prepared to sign up your family, neighbors, pets, businesses and friends for the same trip. I would also have immediately ceased immigration, ceased US financial support to all nations of the world and doubled our military presence and fortifications world-wide.

That would've been my politically incorrect solution. But jebus, what a message we would've sent to Russia, China and every other ass-bag, piss bucket nation who has designs on our way of life. And, what a message that would send to our allies and leech-nations who rely on the US for help and handouts. You want US resources? You want to come here from your shit-pot of a 3rd world donkey corral? You want the protection and security and opportunity provided by US laws, military and society? You had best get in line and be prepared to put some major beans on the table to earn that right.

Anyway, here's another 9/11. I am still pissed. I'll be pissed next year and the year after too. Personally, I am proud that you are an officer in the strongest and most prepared military in history. If the security and strength of my homeland is in the hands of anyone, it would be the hands of the most prepared military man I know. And that's you. You'll be working on the most cutting-edge technology, with the most well-funded labs, with the most brilliant minds in existence today. That's no small feat. That's no small responsibility, either.

Any one of our immediate or extended family could've been on those planes that day, or in those buildings and taken from us by the enemy. I hope you create things that turn the heads of perspective evildoers and makes them say, "Wait, What!? The US can shoot a marble through my skull, right now, from outer space!?"

There's your mission Mike. Protect the US and its people and its pioneer culture. You'll be doing that through the skills, talent and drive you were born with and enabled to hone by the most advanced military organization today.

Stay Strong.
Love,
Dad

That's some strong stuff above and I stand by it. The truth hurts. The truth tends to suck. The truth is, there exist parties out in the world, some parties in strong numbers, who wish us harm. They wish us harm for being US Citizens, Christians, Jews, Muslims, White, Black, Asian, Gay, Weird, Immigrant or what have you. No one is exempt. For the record, I'm in the group that wishes harm on spiders and terrorists. Nobody born human avoids hate. It's just how the human animal interacts. Recognize it. Deal with it.

Buddha would tell us, ***"Silence the angry man with love."*** Now, I'm not Buddha in anything but belly shape so I believe in instruction. The deeper the transgression, the more pointed the instruction. We don't see many lessons being dealt these days and it shows. But that's just me.

I identify very strongly with the US Citizen. My definition is broad and includes everyone here in the US bettering their situation according to our US laws and customs while shedding the crime, poverty, and polarities that drove them here. I believe we have built a free and safe environment where a person can create a family and earn a good living in relative peace and security. I believe we have built this environment on the shoulders of every immigrant who arrived here with nothing but balls and a vision. I believe we built this environment on the backs of every person who arrived here in literal or indentured chains carrying nothing but their precious cultures from around the globe. I believe we built this environment on the stolen, sacred territories of countless indigenous cultures who created trade, law and prosperity throughout the continent 30,000 years before Europe loused up her eastern shores. I believe we built this environment under the protection of a stalwart line of the baddest asses in civil and military history who willingly led and bled at home and overseas so you can watch it on the History Channel from your Barcalounger.

This legacy of blood and dreams demands nothing of you. All are welcome here. That's the beauty of America. That's the truth of America.

Respectfully, I disagree. I say a member is an integral part of the whole. I say this legacy of blood and dreams deserves our respect for its laws and procedures. It deserves our brains and efforts and best work. Our example is the example the newcomers who are dedicated to bettering their situation are witnessing. They should understand that our efforts in nurturing, growth and healing are as critical for the success of the whole as are their efforts. More importantly, our country and all it stands for deserves our protection to ensure it continues.

The ground we stand upon today is soaked in the blood of heroes and buffoons and every person who believed in freedom and society and earning a seat at the table. This is our country. This is our country where Hemmingway would say we are stronger at the places we've been broken. This is our country where every flavor of laborer took their turn building the railroads. This is the country that created the 1992 US Men's Basketball Olympic Dream Team for fuck sakes.

We have a responsibility to protect our country, our community and our family from within while the professionals guard our flanks. That's how men ran their business ever since 3 families first shared a cave. That's how GenX learned how to run things. We looked out for each other. We trusted each other. We worked together. We did our best. We supported our protectors and caregivers. We had fun. We didn't kill each other. We didn't even blame each other. That's the America we need to protect.

Future children deserve the freedom, protection, and

opportunity we've been given. They deserve every opportunity. They deserve the test of their skills. They deserve the rewards of hard work. They need to be able to protect and keep what they've built and earned.

They also need to know that not everyone has their best interests at heart and plan accordingly. They need to know someone somewhere is looking for a free ride on their working backs. They need to know that someone somewhere wishes them harm.

The United States of America is a sensitive machine made of hardened parts. It takes constant maintenance to keep the machine tuned to the current popular whim but the foundation it is built upon remains rock solid, strong and constant.

Despite the ongoing clown-show the nightly news makes us out to be, I have to believe we are all out there doing what's necessary to ensure our personal part of the whole is properly respected, protected, and maintained. End of screed.

*November, 201**

Hi Charlie,

Happy Friday! Looks like you're gonna have a gray and rainy weekend. Same with us. Good weekend to stay in your jammies, sleep and get your studying done. Tomorrow's December. Crazy.

Speaking of crazy, I read an article about a kid who took a pill labeled 'Percocet' at a card game with his friends. His buddy took one as well. They were both stone dead within minutes. The pill was 75% fentanyl. Enough to kill 5 elephants.

I know you're not a stunad about stuff like this but please keep your eyes open and watch out for the other guys who tend to be bozos. There's a lot of stuff out there that'll kill a person who's not paying attention. I want you to live a long, happy and fulfilling life.

Speaking of happy life. It's great work you're doing on the grades and the job search. It will all pay off. It's a long process and it will get scary and frustrating, but you are doing all the right stuff. Hang in and trust the process.

I'm mailing your coat today. You'll need it. Plus, it's a goddamn awesome coat. Your hat and bunny-lined gloves are coming too. Maybe you left a deuce in a pocket.

If it's not raining too bad, Imma do the Christmas lights this weekend. Not my favorite thing, but a good excuse for a corncob and a jar in the garage.

Have a nice weekend.

Be safe.
Love,
Dad

*April, 202**

Hiya Charlie,

2 days left in April 202. Crazy. This year is moving super-fast. It'll be time for the beach before long. Sales on Air Conditioners always happen pre-season, so keep an eye out for deals. Make sure you measure the existing unit. You know it fits.*

I got Paulo to detail Mom's car yesterday. He's usually pretty quiet. This time he talked my ear off non-stop and I had places to be. Here's what I gathered:

He's two weeks into getting divorced. His wife kicked him out because she says he hangs out with known drug dealers. She moved her parents into their house. She's part owner in his business and is trying to eff him up. She's poisoning his kids against him saying he's dangerous and likely to end up in jail. His son is scared shitless of him because of the mom. They both have lawyers now but it's gonna be ugly.

Sooo, I wish them both well. There are always two sides to every story and there's always a backstory to a person's actions. What gets me is the wife poisoning the kids against the dad. That's just mean. And it's bad and wrong as well. Kids need security and peace at home. Kids growing up get barraged by shit from the outside. Bad kids, bad teachers, bad things happening in the world, hard classes, incomprehensible tests, injuries, bad coaches, illness, death and a million other things.

Having a stable, safe and supportive home life is every kid's inalienable right. Unfortunately, a large percentage of parents can't seem to pull their shit together long enough to raise their kids. Most of the time it's just because they are personally motivated.

When you have kids, your personal switch needs to go from internal motivation to external motivation. From 'me' to 'family'. Every decision from that moment on is not for yourself, but for them. Who knows what's going on with Paulo and his wife, but I feel for his kids.

I truly believe you guys are successful products of me and Mom's marriage. We didn't do everything right, but our motivations and actions for the past 25 years were purely for the betterment of our boys and our life as a family unit. Grammy and Old Jim certainly had their moments, but their marriage lasted 62 years and she held his hand as he passed. We should all hope for that brand of constancy and commitment.

I'm writing this all down because my conversation with Paulo bothered me. Their motivation seems vindictive and petty with little thought for their young kids. That's a very immature and internal motivation that just about guarantees ill effects on the kids.

Your motivation to succeed pushed you through the internal, selfish little voices telling you to shirk, ignore or rationalize the hard work, the privation, the stress and the struggle it takes to win. You dug in. You won. That mind-set, that tool-set, that dedication will be integral when you decide to get into a serious relationship and eventually into a marriage and a family of your own.

Relationships take work. Sharing a life with someone is exactly that, sharing a life. Your internal motivations are now external because it's not just you, it's now ya'll. If that is a beneficial union with the right person, you'll change, fight and work hard to keep it functioning smoothly. It's a job with outstanding rewards. Having your mother and you guys changed me in very good ways. It gave me a purpose, direction and focus outside of my own simple shit. It was an avenue of growth with a thousand side ventures of fun, camaraderie and new experiences.

So when you decide it's time to ease into a serious relationship, think of the future. Does this person share the same ideals as me? Do they have a similar background? Do they value family, does their family value family? Do they complement my personality. Do they value my pursuits and what's important to me? Are their goals in line with your goals?

When the situation with a girl clicks and fits like a puzzle piece, you'll know. See past the chemical attraction and the 'new car smell'. See past the dopamine and norepinephrine and picture the future. Do you have enough in common that your path forward is already nicely greased? Do you have nothing in common so every small decision is a fight? Think about it.

So there's my screed on relationships and kids. Having a real partner makes life twice as fun. Having kids turns life on its head and makes it exponentially more fun and more scary. The commitment is real, the job lasts your lifetime and doesn't come with a playbook, the risk exists, but the rewards are endless.

See you at Old Jim's funeral.

Be Good.
Love,

Dad

**"Well, she didn't look as pretty as some others I have known
And she wasn't good at conversation when we were alone
But she had a way of making me believe that I belonged
And it felt like coming home ... when I found her.**

**Cause she seemed to be so proud of me just walking holding hands
And she didn't think that money was the measure of a man
And we seemed to fit together when I held her in my arms
And it left me feeling warm ... when I loved her."**

When I Loved Her - Kris Kristofferson, The Silver-Tongued Devil and I, 1971

I need to step in here at this point. Number one, Kristofferson makes me cry. The lyrics he creates are very simply beautiful. He's the real and a living legend. I highly recommend you revisit his stuff. He's been there. Go see him if he hits your town.

The letter above contains some rare relationship advice to my oldest son. The lovely and elusive Autumn my wife and I have been together for 40 years and married for 34 of those years. We were not a merger. We were a raw start-up, dating in our late teens without 2 nickels to rub together and school loans to look forward to. We know. Relationships take work. You show me an old couple holding hands tottering down the street and I'll show you a monument to grit. Here are two people who had 50 years and 1000 legitimate reasons to kill each other and yet are still watching each other's back. It's a remarkable thing.

As a firmly closeted romantic, this letter presented the practical aspect of relationships to my boy. Hallmark Channel nonsense notwithstanding, lightning will sometimes strike, and you'll find yourself head over heels. If he has the capacity to wait till the smoke clears to assess the situation in real terms as it pertains to the future, so much the better. I know the ladies reading this just sucked the O2 out of North America with the utter lack of romance in that last statement. But I stand by it. Any carpenter will tell you the same thing. A tight-fitting joint will not come apart. Or was that Tommy Chong? Either way, it works.

*December 201**

Hiya my Charlie,

Very nice to have you home. We always sleep better when our boys are safe and under the same roof like the old days.

They id'd that dead kid on the roof downtown, 19-year-old boy from Fairfax, Va. Cops said it's "an isolated instance under investigation". Bottom line, it's pretty easy to die. One wrong move in a car, one wrong step into the street, one night of bad luck in a bar, one poorly swallowed chicken nugget, one bad idea in your head and it's all over.

It's amazing anybody outlives their teen years. I'm glad you're a careful, smart person.

Here are 10 weird things that can kill you almost instantly. Pretty awesome. Watch out for those damn organized cows.

Number 10. <u>A meteor</u>. Humans have been lucky when it comes to avoiding sizeable meteors and mass die-offs. However, if one measuring 50-meters-wide and speeding towards Earth at roughly 9 miles per second exploded in the air, it would be rather catastrophic. The probable effect has been likened to just under 140 atomic bombs going off at once.

Number 9. <u>Stepping on a stonefish</u>. The sea creatures are one of the most poisonous fish. They also really hate it when people step on them. When that happens, the fish immediately release venom into whatever disturbed it.

Effects are fast acting and can include heart stoppage, seizures, and paralysis.

Number 8. <u>Cleaning the toilet</u>. No doubt, it's an item that needs frequent disinfecting, but be very mindful of the products used. Mixing bleach and ammonia results in the formation of a potentially fatal gas.

Number 7. <u>Icicles</u>. They're solid, sharp, and depending upon how far they fall, potentially forceful. On average, the frozen spikes are the agent behind 100 deaths in Russia every year. They have also claimed lives in Chicago, Vermont, and more than one city in Michigan.

Number 6. <u>Too much pumpkin pie and eggnog</u>. In addition to both items being common holiday foods, the two beloved edibles contain nutmeg. The spice, in larger quantities, has a hallucinogenic effect, and when consumed in excess can cause psychosis and death.

Number 5. <u>Underestimating a cow</u>. 22 a year. That is how many annual U.S. fatalities are linked to the often docile-looking animals. Many are due to attacks carried out by a single animal, but bovines have been known to organize and strike in groups.

Number 4. <u>Gamma Ray Bursts</u>. The powerful forces can be released by any number of space objects, but mighty though they are, detection can be difficult. A strike may occur with no advance warning. On the upside, complete annihilation is instantaneous, so victims will likely have spent their final moments in blissful ignorance.

Number 3. <u>Selfies</u>. The popular practice has claimed at least 49 lives over the past couple of years. Most victims fell to their deaths, while others drowned, got struck by trains, were shot, or were involved in a fatal car crash.

Number 2. <u>Rock collecting</u>. The hobby is enjoyed by many, but there are some specimens best avoided. Among them is Hutchinsonite, as inhaling its dust or ingesting bits of it can be fatal. The rock's composition includes 3 deadly minerals – arsenic, lead, and thallium.

Number 1. <u>Eating sushi</u>. If the chef offers you a plate of delicious fugu, get his or her credentials before committing. The blowfish, if not prepared absolutely flawlessly, can kill upon consumption. Just one of them packs enough tetrodotoxin to wipe out 30 people.

Be good, be safe.
Love,
Dad

"The day is necessary
Every now and then
For souls to move on
Given life back again.
Fly on, fly on
Fly on my friend
Go on, live again
Love again."

Life Without You - Stevie Ray Vaughan, Soul to Soul, 1985

"I had seen birth and death but had thought they were different."

- T. S. Eliot

Chapter 15
The Stoic Letters

In my quest to provide the boyos with interesting brain fodder I ran across far more worthy schools of thought and hints for living than I was ever exposed to in my admittedly Catholic focused formative years. The thought of living not under the thumb of an old book or a guy with no kids in ceremonial garb really wasn't an option until we made it out of that circle.

The Vikings tell us in the Bandamanna Saga, " Wisdom is welcome wherever it comes from."

In my perusing, I was happy to find much better ideas about living a good life. What amazed me was the similarities across the ages. In 590 BC, Buddha tells us: ***The secret of health for both mind and body is not to mourn for the past, not to worry about the future, but to live the present moment wisely and earnestly.*** Then, in 60 AD Rome, Seneca comes up with: ***"True happiness is to enjoy the present, without anxious dependence upon the future."*** Tecumseh, The Shawnee Chief in 177something said: ***"Live your life that the fear of death can never enter your heart."***

All of a sudden, it's Ok to enjoy life without worrying about making it past the pearly gates. We have ages of humanity telling us the same thing; to enjoy, to be thoughtful, to not worry about that which may never arrive. The fact is nobody knows what happens after you're gone. What matters is living the day you have in your grasp.

Here's a doosie from Old Tecumseh again:

**"When you rise in the morning...
Give thanks for the light, for your life, for your strength.
Give thanks for your food and for the joy of living.
If you see no reason to give thanks, the fault lies in
yourself."**

Tecumseh, 1768-1813

I would posit that the problem with today's society is encapsulated in the quote above. Too many see no reason to give thanks, no reason to celebrate, no reason to look beyond their own internal "anxious dependance."

I put the blame squarely on the head of the Media. Each media outlet has an ax they want 'We the People' to grind for them, and we are being force-fed worries from every direction we look. We're told that we must be very concerned about that which has zero effect on our daily lives. Their bullshit just ain't true.

The ancients did not worry about the globe. They had life to deal with. Their work helped their immediate community and kinsmen. A final word from Snorre Sturluson puts a cap on it. And Yo, if a guy's name is Snorre, you gotta listen.

**"A foolish man is all night awake, pondering over
everything.
He then grows tired; and when morning comes, all is
lament as before."**
The Elder Edda

If I could have my boys lean toward peace and celebration and away from penance and woe, I'd be providing a better life for them. It was worth a try. After all, it was working for me. If I watch the TV news at all these days, it's just to assess the current shell-game being foisted on the sheep by the Corporation or to see how effectively the weather ladies are matching their outfits to the forecast slides.

And by the way, from the Native Americans to the Vikings, to the Greek and Roman Philosophers to the Asian Philosophers; all believed in an afterlife where we will happily greet our ancestors, families, and friends.

The big difference? In those schools of thought, no payment is required to get there.

*April, 202**

Hiya Mikey,

Happy mid-April. Hot, cold, wet, blowy, dark and sunny all in the same 1/2 hour. It was a fun weekend hosting you and the team! It was great to see you and the team playing and relaxing. Enormous amounts of food. The house was serviceable and close enough to the fields. We are fortunate to be able to do things like that occasionally. Most ain't. Some can but don't.

Anyway, I started a new book of Seneca's letters to somebody. I'm finding the Stoics have an excellent world/life view that resonates more with me than the Catholic teachings I was bludgeoned with for most of my life.

Here's some quotes from Seneca:

- *Religion is regarded by the common people as true, by the wise as false, and by the rulers as useful.*
- *He who is brave is free.*
- *Life, if well lived, is long enough.*
- *Wherever there is a human being, there is an opportunity for a kindness.*
- *It is quality rather than quantity that matters.*
- *A gem cannot be polished without friction, nor a man perfected without trials.*
- *True happiness is... to enjoy the present, without anxious dependence upon the future.*
- *The wish for healing has always been half of health.*
- *All cruelty springs from weakness.*

- *The greatest remedy for anger is delay.*
- *If you wished to be loved, love.*
- *One must steer, not talk.*

How great is this guy!? Common sense without the collection basket. Tips on being a content and productive human during your lifetime. I was taught that life is suffering, and you better hope you get into heaven so you can finally rest.

The idea that a life, well-lived, is enough, is a very freeing concept for an old lapsed catholic like meself. I work for a good day, not a good afterlife. After all, no one knows what will happen after. So take some direction from one, two or a few of the above.

Read the Marcus Aurelius' book you got for Christmas. His whole gist: "Remember that very little is needed to make a happy life."

Stay Strong,
Love,
Dad

Time for another GenX public service announcement. You've lasted this long, it'll be OK.

We see a bunch of pissed-off people today. More pissed-off people than we've seen in a long time. Why? Because pissed-off sells.

Pissed-off outsells scared.

Righteous indignation is fun. Circling up your like-minded comrades and lighting emoji torches for your dictated enemy-of-the-week passes as socializing these days. Pissed-off is encouraged by all the media outlets. It's as obvious as the June spike in gas prices and just as pitiful. Come on folks. GenX is watching you all get played like that stupid electric fiddle Little Busey was playing on Starship Troopers and it's just as embarrassing.

Seneca says, *The greatest remedy for anger is delay.*

Pick your fights. Consider your fights. Take your time, gather some real data and be discerning about your pet causes before donning your immolation robes and dousing your fleece with coal-oil and misinformation. It just makes good sense. Know who you're helping. Know if you even should be helping.

*July, 202**

Hiya Mike,

Nothing like a seven-week hiatus in your letters! Many things went on. It was great having you home. It was great seeing you travel and relax and laugh. The highlights for me: playing cards on the porch down the shore and burying 2 Mack's pies.

Having a few weeks working back at the Academy campus is a great way to practice living on your own, marshalling your time, planning things to do, eat, see and enjoy. While getting paid!

The fact that people knew your schedule and knew when you were coming back in order to pull you back into your research is remarkable. That means you've already earned respect in the scientific community. Your attitude, work ethic and smarts will always create a smooth road for you to follow.

So here we are knocking on the door to August. This year has moved unbelievably fast. Today is the last Friday I'll be working. I start working M, T, W next week. It's going to be very strange.

I started working for real in 1976 when I was 11. I got a cash-paying job working in the business office of The Local Rectory, where the priests live. The office was on the first floor with the library and the kitchen. People would come in looking for a priest or call in needing to schedule a memorial mass or include petitions for Sunday or get a Baptismal

Certificate or drop off donations. Sometimes it would be a food delivery or piece of furniture that I'd have to carry. Most of the time, it was the beer delivery. Lugging multiple cases of beer up the steps to the priests' rooms was just tiring and heavy.

But the best part was on payday. Going to the giant 5-foot-high, bronze wall safe to collect my little, brown envelope. There would be coins in the envelope and a few bills. Maybe $15 bucks plus if it was a busy week.

I never let go of the pleasure of making money. I was a natural Ebenezer back then, hoarding my cash in a secret box in my room. Counting it all the time. Thinking of all the things I could get with my money. I still have a deep appreciation for the value of work, the value of service, the value of money husbandry but I'll never forget the day I was worth a solid $60 for the first time ever.

The value of money is simply a better life. I would be out playing street hockey with 10 other kids from the neighborhood, and we'd ride our bikes to the shopping center for food. They'd be counting their change and bumming quarters trying to make up the $2.50 for a slice and a coke. I'd whip out a knot and grab 2 slices and still have quarters for the Galaga machine. My money, well spent.

Remember pizza after guitar lessons? That's some great stuff. That's me at my most content: my boys, my 'zah, a free Saturday afternoon to relax.

That's my Stoic-leaning idea of a better life. Squared away small stuff equals less worry about the big stuff. A better life doesn't require a shitload of money. It only requires 'enough'. The good news is, YOU get to decide what's enough. Back then, 'enough' for me was an extra slice and a video game. Today, 'enough' for me is a whole pie and a card game. Keep your 'enoughs' in order, and you'll be juuust fine.

Wealth is the slave of a wise man. The master of a fool. —
Seneca

Anyway, welcome back to the letters! Enjoy your time working. The rewards are never just monetary.

Stay Strong
Love,
Dad

So, let the evidence show that my idea of a good life, even from way back when, is Pizza and a Game. I'll own that all day long and die a happy man. That simply means happiness is always within my grasp or I'm just really easy to please. They both work.

The letter coming up is a rare "Boyz" missive to both my sons. One Christmas I gave them each their own copy of Meditations by Marcus Aurelius. Am I a fun Dad or what? Fun as a chipped tooth they'd no doubt tell you. As you read the excerpts from Meditations below, you'll see why I felt they should have a hard copy to wear out.

Here we have a ruling Emperor of Rome who, while RULING the EMPIRE OF ROME took the time to jot down his thoughts on being the real. His thoughts on morality and purpose resonated immediately. I found the whole thing remarkable enough to share. The following letter baited the hook. It was also the first appearance of The Code.

*February, 202**

Hi my Boyz,

Happy February. Imbolc. The mid-point between winter and spring solstices. The earth's teetering between sleep and waking up. This is the time that things begin to change.

For those of you who haven't read your Marcus Aurelius books. Here's where he's coming from. With locations no less. Every one of these quotes is worth a few moments to consider and internalize. Pick a few and add to your code.

You don't have a code you live by? Might be time to make one of your own. Here's the Marcus with some insight:

- *"The others obey their own lead, follow their own impulses. Don't be distracted. Keep walking. Follow your own nature, and follow Nature—along the road they share." (5.3)*

- *"What injures the hive injures the bee." (6.54)*

- *"Indifference to external events. And a commitment to justice in your own acts. Which means: thought and action resulting in the common good. What you were born to do." (9.31)*

- *"When you wake up in the morning, tell yourself: The people I deal with today will be meddling, ungrateful, arrogant, dishonest, jealous, and surly. They are like this because they can't tell good from evil. But I have seen the beauty of good, and the ugliness of evil, and have recognized that the wrongdoer has a nature related to my own—not of the same blood or birth, but the same mind, and possessing a share of the divine." (2.1)*

- *"People who labor all their lives but have no purpose to direct every thought and impulse toward are wasting their time—even when hard at work." (2.7)*

- *"At dawn, when you have trouble getting out of bed, tell yourself: 'I have to go to work—as a human being. What do I have to complain of, if I'm going to do what I was born for— the things I was brought into the world to do? Or is this what I was created for? To huddle under the blankets and stay warm?'" (5.1)*

- *"Perfection of character: to live your last day, every day, without frenzy, or sloth, or pretense." (7.69)*

- *"The things you think about determine the quality of your mind. Your soul takes on the color of your thoughts." (5.16)*

- *"The mind in itself has no needs, except for those it*

creates itself. Is undisturbed, except for its own disturbances. Knows no obstructions, except those from within." (7.16)

- *"Choose not to be harmed— and you won't feel harmed. Don't feel harmed and you haven't been." (4.7)*

- *"Objective judgment, now, at this very moment. Unselfish action, now, at this very moment. Willing acceptance—now, at this very moment—of all external events. That's all you need." (9.6)*

- *"External things are not the problem. It's your assessment of them. Which you can erase right now." (8.47)*

- *"Your three components: body, breath, mind. Two are yours in trust; to the third alone you have clear title." (12.3)*

- *"To stop talking about what the good man is like, and just be one." (10.16)*

- *"Be satisfied with even the smallest progress and treat the outcome of it all as unimportant." (9.29)*

- *"Most of what we say and do is not essential. If you can eliminate it, you'll have more time, and more tranquillity. Ask yourself at every moment, 'Is this necessary?'" (4.24)*

- *"The impediment to action advances action. What stands in the way becomes the way." (5.20)*

- *"To bear in mind constantly that all of this has happened before. And will happen again—the same plot from beginning to end, the identical staging. Produce them in your mind, as you know them from experience or from history…All just the same. Only the people different." (10.27)*

- *"Forget everything else. Keep hold of this alone and remember it: Each of us lives only now, this brief instant. The rest has been lived already or is impossible to see." (3.10)*

Anyway, my boyos, if everyone approached life with these concepts in mind, the world would be a nicer, calmer, more productive place. Your good actions impact the hive. Your internal peace spreads to the others. These things are not done for a happy afterlife, but for a happy today.

I wish you both a happy today. Like Marcus says, the past is done, the future ain't here yet.
Love,
   Dad

*March, 202**

Hey There Mikey,

It was nice to see you on the call yesterday. You look healthy and bright-eyed.

Yeah. It's kinda disappointing that you are not getting the interaction and comradery that you are used to getting coming from a world-class military academy, but guess what? Most of life is like that anyway. You fend for yourself and hope for the best. You hope you have the intellect, the will, the motivation, the time and the resources to do your job, to live, to prosper. It's a crap-shoot that favors the prepared. You, The Mike, are certainly prepared.

You're also a product of your environment. Mc's of our branch tend to enjoy and thrive in a self-sustaining environment. Social activities are generally viewed as required, not entertainment. We make our own fun. Always have. You're just doing what we do. And doing well. We know that problems tend to arise due to other people not due to us. We just have to deal with the fallout. The fact is, you're better off concentrating on your job because people are troubles 85% of the time.*

So don't fret. You're a friggin stand-alone pillar of survival and excellence. You created everything around you including a clear path forward. Enjoy it! You've already aced half this UK thing and the clock's ticking. Savor your very comfortable personal hidey hole where nobody can bother you this year. You will remember it fondly when you're 3 nipples deep in annoying people issues in the future. Keep your resume updated.

Here's 2 Marcus Aurelius quotes I like:

Never let the future disturb you. You will meet it, if you have to, with the same weapons of reason which today arm you against the present.

Perfection of character is this: to live each day as if it were your last, without frenzy, without apathy, without pretense.

Have a good week my boy.

Stay Strong.
Love,
Dad

Aaaand, kindly allow one of the philosophical virtuosos of GenX to sum it all up.

"Don't take life too seriously. You'll never get out alive!"

— Bugs Bunny

My beloved lets get down to business
Mental self defensive fitness
Don't rush the show
You gotta go for what you know
Make everybody see, in order to fight the powers that be."

Fight the Power – Public Enemy, Fear of a Black Planet, 1989

Chapter 16
Seasons

This is a longer chapter and I'm not entirely sure why the changing of the seasons pushes me into a contemplative frame of mind. I inherited the ability to sense the seasonal changes from my mother, but it is very difficult to explain. By necessity in the northern climes, people needed to work hand in hand with the seasons to endure and thrive. Somewhere down the line they became attuned. The seasons are never as static as our calendars would indicate. They tend to be just a bit offset from our religious and cultural holidays that mark the flow of time.

My mother, usually around late July or early August, would sniff deeply, look at the sky, study the wind in the leaves and proclaim summer to be over. In that moment, Summer would have crested and began its subsidence into Fall. We could all feel it and understood exactly what she was saying in our core. To this day, my mom and siblings know when a change is gonna come.

"Woo-hoo, witchy woman
See how high she flies
Woo-hoo, witchy woman
She got the moon in her eye."

Witchy Woman – Eagles, Eagles, 1972

She gave a meaning to that undefinable melancholic tweak to the subconscious that some of us feel when the breeze hints bittersweet and subtly changes its tone and pitch in preparation for…something.

The sun and scents of the seasons are different and obvious. However, the way the sun, scents and wind change from one term to the other is very subtle. This is where we find ourselves in this chapter. Our nose to the air, fine-tuned to the shifting of the seasons and all the feels they bring.

"We had joy, we had fun,
We had seasons in the sun,
But the hills that we climbed,
Were just seasons out of time."

Seasons in the Sun – Terry Jacks, Seasons in the Sun, 1973

*January, 202**

Hiya Mike,

Happy New Year! Big stuff. Eh. I never really got a Calendar-based holiday. I like to celebrate the seasons, recognize the Solstices, take my living cues from nature.

To me, Winter equals regrouping, sheltering, regeneration. Spring equals cleaning out, shedding dead-weight (physical, mental, stuff and otherwise), scrubbing up and emerging back into society and full productivity. Summer equals energy, growth, everything doing their job and most of all the sun powering everything into a frenzy of flowers, fruit, bugs, waves and wind.

Autumn, however, is the prize in my view. Fall is the culmination of all the work and energy spent. It's when the only work left is to gather the fruit. It's when the earth takes a deep breath, surveys the bounty of the year and prepares to rest.

That's me. The beauty of the seasons is that you can impart your own meaning to the cycle. Make the turning of time work for you by creating your own rituals, your own meaning, your own action and philosophy.

Here's some thoughts from brainy folk:

I believe in process. I believe in four seasons. I believe that winter's tough, but spring's coming. I believe that there's a growing season. You realize that in life, if you grow, you get better. Steve Southerland

I need the seasons to live to the rhythm of rain and sun. Sophie Marceau

The coming and going of the seasons give us more than the springtime, summers, autumns, and winters of our lives. It reflects the coming and going of the circumstances of our lives like the glassy surface of a pond that shows our faces radiant with joy or contorted with pain. Gary Zukav

Yes sir, I am a tortured man for all seasons, as they say, and I have powerful friends in high places. Birds sing where I walk, and children smile when they see me coming.

Hunter S. Thompson

The best thing about a British winter is the cold weather, real fires, frosty mornings. I love living somewhere that has proper seasons. Jane Fallon

To be interested in the changing seasons is a happier state of mind than to be hopelessly in love with spring. George Santayana

When the seasons shift, even the subtle beginning, the scent of a promised change, I feel something stir inside me. Hopefulness? Gratitude? Openness? Whatever it is, it's welcome. Kristin Armstrong

I like dressing in all seasons. Every season has its own character and charm. Pierce Brosnan

You know yourself; you gotta know your seasons. There be certain seasons, it's telepathy. Ghostface Killah

For millions of years, this world has been a great gift to nearly everything living on it, a planet whose atmosphere, temperature, air, water, seasons, and weather were precisely calibrated to allow us - the big us, including forests and oceans, species large and small - to flourish. Rebecca Solnit

Anyway, welcome to the Winter. Enjoy the season!

Stay Strong.
Love,
Dad

*April, 202**

Hey There Mike,

Happy Tuesday in April. Probably the most useless of months running neck and neck with March. If March is the Shemp of Months, April is definitely the Curly Joe. April's the black jellybean in the Easter Basket. If you make your favorite month the filet mignon of the year, March is Spam and April is a chicken dog.

It'll be nice to get the trees nice and leafy again blocking the new development out back but the accompanying snuzzles are killing us. We had a nice Easter dinner at Micky's. Burgers and dogs. Everybody's doing well.

I thought about what you said the other day, that your life will be spent solitary like this year. I don't think so. You will likely work in the US, on a team, in a non-academic environment. There will be people with common interests. There will be sports to play, gyms, movies, restaurants. There will be military, like-minded people who know the ropes. It'll get better.

Here are some thoughts from folks who have been there too:

- *"Music was my refuge. I could crawl into the space between the notes and curl my back to loneliness." — Maya Angelou*
- *"Sometimes you need to be alone. Not to be lonely, but to enjoy your free time being yourself." — Anonymous*
- *"The greatest thing in the world is to know how to*

belong to oneself." —*Michel de Montaigne*
- "*All great and precious things are lonely.*" —*John Steinbeck*
- "*The soul that sees beauty may sometimes walk alone.*" —*Johann Wolfgang Von Goethe*
- "*A season of loneliness and isolation is when the caterpillar gets its wings. Remember that next time you feel alone.*" —*Mandy Hale*
- "*Sometimes you have to stand alone just to make sure you still can.*" —*Anonymous*
- "*Sometimes you need to take a break from everyone and spend time alone to experience, appreciate, and love yourself.*" —*Robert Tew*

Anyway, you're rocking your first assignment so keep on rocking. You know what works for you. You know how to do. You know how to excel. You know how to win.

That's 90% of the puzzle. You have plenty of time to work out the remaining 10%.

I hope your April is a quick one leading into your birthday month!

Stay Strong.
Love,
Dad

*Early November 201**

Hiya my Charlie,

Fall is finally here. Fall is your old Dad's favorite time of year. August and September are rife with the angst of cramming in that last taste of vacation and gathering school supplies and class schedules. Even so many years removed from going to class myself, I still get that ice ball in my stomach and have those dreams where I can't find my homeroom or I'm late for an exam for a class I never attended.

Our grade schools and high schools were mean, crowded, shit shows. 30 kids to a class (75% were Irish working-class brawling knuckleheads), over-worked and under-paid teachers with very little talent or enthusiasm, bitter nuns and priests trained in punishment and snark. I always dreaded August and hated September.

But then there's October. October is when nature realizes the big winter sleep is imminent and cuts loose with a final display of power and beauty. Every leaf is a bright and miniature mural, red berries erupt onto the evergreens, drying summer grasses throw tall shoots of swaying purple fronds that wave goodbye to warm summer evenings and hello to arctic blasts that send maelstroms of leaves up and away.

The woodsmoke of autumn, the high, honking geese overhead, the cider-scented wind in rapidly baring orchard branches, the slant of the sun that's not summer yet not quite winter but a changing constant, reflecting clouds across stubble-fields on an afternoon drive. Fall settles like an old friend in your comfy chair. Fall is confident. It knows what's coming and is serene in its culmination.

Autumn knows that the damp brashness of Spring and the hectic tumescence of Summer can't hold a candle to the golden harvest in her patched pockets, her dwindling daylight and the wind-driven clouds that never quite obscure the Hunter's Moon. Autumn is nostalgic and significant in ways the other seasons can only aspire.

Autumn wind and Autumn sun are gifts. Autumn is meant to be enjoyed outdoors and all senses are meant to be employed in its appreciation. So go grab you some Fall. If you believe, like I do, that trees are just animals that move verrrry slowly, grab a seat beneath one and feel its weight, its resignation and contentment to drift into a long winter's nap.

Autumn is a cycle that ushers us into our own chill period.

Winter is enforced time spent indoors, low lighting with hot tea and a book while sleet batters the windows. Autumn, however, invites you outside to witness her aging splendor and dignified end to the year's journey. Autumn invites you to bathe in her crisp air while gust-chased leaves accumulate at your feet. Her only wish: that her fading light warms your face for a fleeting, final moment.

To some, Fall is football. To me, Fall is nature saying thank you to those who can appreciate it.

Be safe.
Love,
Dad

OK, Hank Thoreau, calm down.

*November 201**

Hiya my Charlie,

Happy November. The kickoff to Holiday Season. The time of year when the weather gets chilly and people get warm with the winter spirit. We give thanks to the Summer for the growth and energy leading to Autumn's harvest. We give thanks for the bounty of food our efforts have supplied. We take comfort in our families and friends. We celebrate the successful closing of another cycle. We celebrate the opportunity to rest and recover and regroup for the next year.

In the old days, winter was the time for leisurely mending our tools, clothes, hurts and property. People, tucked away by a snug fire, reading, playing music, chatting while socks were being mended, fishing nets re-strung, sickles sharpened, stew bubbling, coffee brewing, while the winter gradually took hold, winds rattling old shutters, ponds icing over, livestock in their warm barns eating the freshly mown hay first.

We've lost the enforced down-time winter creates and it's a shame. It's something that's in the blood of the northern tribes. I know I feel it every year. The winding down, the falling leaves, the shorter days. It all calls me toward a fire and a drink and a book and some music. If the Summer is buzzing with sun, growth and life, the Winter is the patter of sleet on a frosted window, winter whistling through naked branches and small critters sleeping warm in their burrows a foot beneath the snow.

So as we ease into the season, try to ease some blank space into your day. Try to ease some ease into your schedule. Block off a solid evening or 2 per week from 5 to 10 to do something for yourself even if that something is absolutely nothing. Maybe you have an evening for a nice dinner, a slow perusal of the local vinyl shop and a nightcap by your turntable with a couple candles and a tumbler of quality rum. Maybe you hike through the woods and fields feeling the crunch of leaves under your feet with the scent of wood smoke and pine easing the work grind from your brain.

We're kicking off the Holiday Season. It's your season to slow down. It's your season to sit back and contemplate the fading year and all its victories and disappointments. It's your humanity-granted privilege to take the necessary time to regroup, reassess and restore your depleted energy reserves. Restring your nets, sharpen your knives, organize your workshop, sing, eat, drink and welcome the opportunity to celebrate your year, your life.

You made it. It's time to enjoy a little peace and warmth and quiet celebration in your snug and securely locked burrow in the borough.

Be good.
Love,
Dad

*January 202**

Hiya Charlie,

Very nice to see you last night! You look great. Fit and happy. Happy Winter. We're into it now. Finally. A nice artic blast is blowing in tonight pushing temps into the single digits and wind chills below zero. The big snowstorm we were supposed to get on Sunday night they just turned it to 1 inch of snow turning into hours of rain. Boo. Cicely my ass. She's gotta fix her forecasting wingdingle.

Anyway, this is the time of year we get to hunker down unapologetically in the cozy spots of our own choosing while the elephants whistle outside. I like lamplight and books and hot tea. And now you have the choicest of spaces where you can settle in and winter awhile. Those thick walls are the perfect thing for cozy.

Here's some winter insights:

- *Winter is a season of recovery and preparation.*
  Paul Theroux
- *In the depth of winter I finally learned that there was in me an invincible summer.*
  Albert Camus
- *It is the life of the crystal, the architect of the flake, the fire of the frost, the soul of the sunbeam. This crisp winter air is full of it.*
  John Burroughs
- *In winter, I plot and plan. In spring, I move.*
  Henry Rollins
- *I prefer winter and fall, when you feel the bone structure of the landscape. Something waits beneath it; the whole story doesn't show.*
  Andrew Wyeth
- *The pine stays green in winter... wisdom in hardship.*
  Norman Douglas
- *And finally Winter, with its bitin', whinin' wind, and*

all the land will be mantled with snow.
Roy Bean

- *While I relish our warm months, winter forms our character and brings out our best.*
Tom Allen

Our little Christmas Tree is happy and green in the back. I think he liked being planted in the mild wet weather we had during the break. You wouldn't believe the billions of needles it lost when we moved it. But it's looks good now. Yon doogan is liking sitting on the hill and watching the builders through the woods now that the leaves are gone. The lights are down, the wreaths are packed, our new windows are keeping the house cozy. Your brother is doing well. All is right with the world.

So, have yourself a winter. Make quiet time for yourself. Sharpen your weapons, mend your nets, eat your root veggies, mull your cider and warm your gullet, read for fun, spin quality tunes by lamplight.

Like Henry Rollins says, plot and plan for the spring. This is our time.

Be Good.
Love,
Dad

*February, 202**

Hiya my Charlie,

Happy HumpDay. Here we are in the thick of the work season. Holidays done. New Years done. Back-to-work done. Nothing now but to get to it and make hay. It'll be balls to the wall until we start hearing about college spring breaks, baseball spring training and Easter. Then it'll get warm, muddy and gross.

I actually like it when things normalize into a coherent schedule. Disruption is an excuse for most slackers to continue slacking. When things start to hum and people achieve their groove, shit gets done. Don't be afraid to point people in the right direction to get shit done better.

I'm happy to hear your list of home projects. Every small job competed is victory for your health and well-being. You've got time to chip away at them and the funds will come for the bigger ones. Live below your means for good piece of mind.

Here's some wisdom around home ownership:

"It's easy to underestimate the real cost of home ownership." - Suze Orman

"If I were asked to name the chief benefit of the house, I should say: the house shelters daydreaming, the house protects the dreamer, the house allows one to dream in peace." — Gaston Bachelard

"The ache for home lives in all of us, the safe place where we can go as we are and not be questioned." — Maya Angelou

"You can't have everything you want, but you can have the things that really matter to you." — Marissa Mayer

"I never truly understood the meaning of warmth until I purchased my own home. As I sit in my own living room, surrounded by walls painted my favorite color, looking out at the mighty oak tree sitting on the lot I so carefully chose and listening to the tranquil sounds of jazz music on my stereo, my soul is filled with deep contentment, a warmth that I could not before have fathomed." - Marshall Field

"Everyone desires to own their own home, but the actual purchase is usually reserved for those with work ethic, who are brave and committed." - Louis Glickman

Have a nice day! Sunny and cold. Just the way we like it.

Be good.
Love,
Dad

If you've been paying any attention at all, you're aware that Spring just ain't my time of year. Bad enough to make me wax poetic. Again. Don't say I didn't warn you.

*Mid-March, 202**

Hiya Charlie,

Looks like we're officially into Springtime. I love the changing seasons and would never willingly want to live where it's always hot, but I don't like the Spring. Summer's nice, Fall and Winter are great, but then comes Spring.

Wet, muddy, humid, buggy, allergies. Cold, hot, windy, steamy, longer daylight, school, Easter, final exams, busy workdays. It's a headlong rush to get through annoying Spring into relaxing Summer.

Spring's a transition month. Just like the Fall only with no class, gravitas or sparkle in her eye. Spring's all about an exploding landscape, buds, blooms, bug hatches and babies. You can practically hear the plants screaming in pain as they bust open trying to pollinate and catch some sun to continue living. I used to enjoy the Spring Soccer seasons, you guys running around in your new spikes. New spikes that only were good for 1 season since your feet grew so fast. The start of the Baseball season was always nice at PenCo Field.

They say shit like, rebirth, reawakening, the earth rising from her dormancy, yeah, it's all of that and it's amazing. But, to me, it's the forced expulsion from my Winter Haven, my personal secluded cold weather den where my fire, tea, books and music live. Spring was always time to clean and tune the lawn mower, spread weed control and fertilizer, spray for bugs and a thousand other chores that were shelved in Winter.

Although we never stopped working through the Winter, Spring always seems to yell, "Get back to work!" And for that alone, I say Spring can kiss my balz.

Anyway, you are working on almost a full year on your own, in your own house, bossing your own job, working your own schedule and living the life of your design. I'm proud to see you settle into your life. You're keeping focused, you're keeping fit, you're keeping your possessions curated and maintained, you're keeping productive and essential at work, you're basically living and winning big.

Don't ever doubt or take for granted what got you here. It wasn't us, it wasn't the doogan, or school, the New Testament or Fortune Cookie contents. It was all you. Your work ethic, your incredible intelligence, your sensitive heart and soul, your drive for excellence, your compassion, your sharp memory of the good and your discarding of the bad. You've done well.

And now Spring is telling you to kick it up a notch. Well, fuck Spring. You don't have to kick anything up a notch. You've earned the right to live at your pace, change and grow at your pace and add or subtract whatever the hell you would like to add or subtract to your life.

It's a nice, secure and comforting place to be. So, your assignment is to enjoy what you've accomplished and tell Spring to mind her own business.

Be Good.
Love,
Dad

I notice my Fuck-it List continues to grow faster than my Bucket List. Analyze that.

*June 202**

Hiya my Charlie,

Happy June! Gateway to summer. Wet to warm weather. Flowers, birds and breezes. My Birthday month. End of school month. Father's Day month. Winding down month. Start of the vacation season.

Time to pull back a bit from the work and the deadlines and ease some space and downtime into your routine. Time to enjoy the outside and air out the inside. Physically and metaphorically.

Here's some summer wisdom:

• Rest is not idleness, and to lie sometimes on the grass under trees on a summer's day, listening to the murmur of the water, or watching the clouds float across the sky, is by no means a waste of time. John Lubbock

• Summer afternoon, summer afternoon; to me those have always been the two most beautiful words in the English language. Henry James

• Deep summer is when laziness finds respectability. Sam Keen

• What is one to say about June, the time of perfect young summer, the fulfillment of the promise of the earlier months, and with as yet no sign to remind one that its fresh young beauty will ever fade. Gertrude Jekyll

• Oh, the summer night, Has a smile of light, And she sits on a sapphire throne. Bryan Procter

• Summer is the annual permission slip to be lazy. To do nothing and have it count for something. To lie in the grass and count the stars. To sit on a branch and study the clouds. Regina Brett

• It will not always be summer; build barns. Hesiod

• Once something has outlived its usefulness in one area of life, its purpose for being in existence is no longer the same. The leaf that captures a stream of sunlight, and then transfers its energy to the tree, serves one purpose in the spring and summer, and another completely different one through the fall and winter. Guy Finley

- *'Tis now the summer of your youth: time has not cropped the roses from your cheek, though sorrow long has washed them. Edward Moore*

So, enjoy the summer my Charlie. You've got the employment, coin and security to work some fun into your life. Work some slow-down into your days and admire the small stuff, appreciate your co-workers, hit an early happy hour, find a comfy chair under a tree or on the beach. Every June is a surprise.
You rule.

Be good.
Love,
Dad

*June, 202**

Hey There, my Mikey,

Happy Summer Solstice. Longest day of the year as Pop would tell us every year. This is the official start of the summer according to astronomy. I wonder if you'll see any woowoo Druid activity over there. We have a nice grey day today. Big rain on its way tonight. That got me off the hook for watering all our stuff yesterday. Mom's in Vienna all this week. She fit 7 work outfits into her carry-on suitcase. It was impressive. Probably had the density of lead and the potential explosive energy of a stick of dynamite.

All I can tell you about working in the summer, is that people move slower, people are not around when you need them, stuff doesn't get signed, deliveries take longer and heat makes folks grumpy.

Take all that, fold in your extreme mental and physical work ethic and plan accordingly. Extend your timelines a wee. Be prepared for delays. Ratchet down your hurry. Eat fruit. Have some summer fun. Build in some gaps in your schedule so you can travel around and see some stuff. Stonehenge today would have been cool.

I can't believe I haven't seen you since Christmas. That's 6 months. Too long a time for a boy not to see the face of his father. But, we'll see you soon. Think about being patient and gracious and happy with us when we do. It's totally against our natural bearing and state of mind, I know, but make the effort for your Mother's sake.

Plan on a day out with your brother, hopefully playing some golf. He hasn't done anything about St Andrews yet. He spent 14 hours at work yesterday. It might be a beau geste if you attempt to schedule something yourself. We are using Wed for the Loch Ness/Highlands trip.

Yesterday was the day 2 white peahens appeared in the back yard.

I was looking out my work window and saw something big and white down at the salt lick. I thought it was a plastic bag or balloons or something so I went out to get it. As I got closer, it became 2 white things. Then it became 2 beautiful snow-white lady peacocks. When I said, "Hello ladies!" They bounced over the fence into the yard and started coming toward me like they expected food. No tags, cuffs or bands on them. They were fascinated by the pool and spent time wandering the patio. I had to get back to work and didn't see them leave, but the preacher's wife around the bend had them in her yard shortly after according to the FizzBook. It was totally cool. Very auspicious.

Charlie says, it's either a really good omen, or a really bad omen.........I'm opting for good.

Have a nice remainder of the week my boy.

Stay Strong.
Love,
Dad

*August, 202**

Hiya the Charlie,

Into the dog days now.

We've all been indoctrinated to hustle and achieve. But the reality is that your definition of success is what matters most. My treadmill isn't yours to climb on, neither is anyone else's idea of success yours to pursue.

You've spent blood, sweat and tears defining your personal brand of success. You've achieved so much over the years that a chance to regroup, slow down, consider the wide world and enjoy life is yours to pluck.

Summertime is always a good time to smell the roses. I'm glad you'll be doing some travelling with work and play. Glad you have a solid home-base to hang your hat. Glad you are healthy and able to smile, laugh and test yourself in strength and fitness.

Slowing down a bit lets you keep and tune your focus. In other words, ya'll can't think when it's too noisy and you're running around. Summers are for shade and deep thoughts with an icy beverage. Glad you have the opportunity to exercise the right.

So have a good week. Say a prayer that Mom's gizzards don't equal anything needing further treatment.

Love,
Dad

*July, 202**

Hi There Mikey,

Happy Lughnasa. The Celtic beginning of the harvest season starts between 29th and the 1st. It's seen as the beginning of Autumn. It's seen as the end of the 'hungry season' with bread, berries and food in abundance.

So this is your time to celebrate the fruits of your labor. Find a local Holy Well (there's gotta be one somewhere) and put some flowers on it. Bake a loaf or a cake to celebrate your work and accomplishments. Find some fresh fruit to celebrate another successful growing season for you and the earth.

The future may be uncertain, but today, you have your work, your growth and your awesomeness to celebrate. This year's natural production has peaked. Fruit is pickable, flowers harvestable, robin's eggs hatched, fawns born. And yet, you're not close to peaking. Amazing. No better way to celebrate than gifting yourself some freedom to roam and explore and dig into your surroundings before you find your new assignment.

It was great to see you in Scotland. You look healthy, strong, sharp and focused. You look like a dude who could run a mile up-hill, fight a mountain lion and write a funny limerick about it on the walk home.

Let us know when you hear about your next steps. It will work out the way it is meant to work out so don't fret. You are well prepared for whatever they put on your plate and wherever that plate is set. It will be an adventure. An adventure served up to a man who's ready and capable. This is the stuff life is made of.

Stay Strong.
Love,
Dad

"… Seasons change with the scenery
Weavin' time in a tapestry
Won't you stop and remember me?"

Hazy Shade of Winter – The Bangles, Less Than Zero, 1987

Chapter 17
Stuff You Need to Know
But Nobody Will Tell You

If any chapter of this book riles folks, it'll be this one. I look around me and see all kinds of people who, at some point, needed better information. I see people who needed an honest answer and never got one. GenX has no issue with honesty. In fact, the more brutal the honesty the better.

The Vapors said it very well way back in 1980. Yeah, 1980. Still works.

"Don't like your plastic shoes
Don't like your hair dyed blue
Don't like your damned new rose
Don't like your casual pose
I don't wanna go out tonight
But I don't wanna sit here 'cause there's nothing on the
radio
You're coming 'round tonight
In your parachute suit that you bought in Portobello."

Spring Collection – The Vapors, New Clear Days, 1980

A guy in the back is asking for an example of honest feedback.
Off the of my head, sir. Behold a niece in her teens:
"Whaddya think about my new nose piercing, Dad?"
"Well, Enid, it looks like you've got a bunger hanging out of your nose.
It's distracting and kinda gross. I really don't need to look at that before dinner.

Wait, wait! On second thought, maybe you could hang your car keys off that thing so you won't lose them EVERY FIVE GODDAMN MINUTES!"

The result? She frumped away muttering and he never saw the nose thing again. Would she wear it to school? Probably. Would her mom tell her it's Ok for casual stuff but not professional? Yes. Would they ever hear about piercings again? I doubt it. Would it show up on a job interview? No, it wouldn't.

Thanks for the question.

Kids are gonna do their thing and that's fine. But they deserve to know the reality of some actions from a cost/benefit perspective. Honesty is never easy and fun. In fact, it very rarely is anything but a harsh eye-opener. Kids deserve to know that "the folly of youth" is real and the missteps will reverberate into the future. They need to be aware that the concept of "Standing Out in the Crowd" turned from class and professionalism to a side-show somewhere along the line. Stand-outs were known for excellence, not for shock factor.

GenX excelled at flying under the radar. Acres of ink, nose holes and flappy ears we don't get. Those physical scars, burns, breaks, punctures, and road rashes garnered in our GenX youth were real and manifested later in life as constant aches. Nobody warned us, either. We didn't pay for our body modifications with money. We paid with surprise and pain and had to endure the laughter and ridicule of our friends when it happened. We have that durn lumbago to prove it. The mental scars from those days faded while the lessons remained and never slowed our roll. GenX isn't gonna pull into the afterlife on a golden escalator. We're gonna slide our V8 Interceptor into the pearly gates sideways and toss Pete a Bartles and Jaymes wine cooler.

The culture we see advertised today does not take into account the benefits of responsibility and community GenX learned. We are firmly ensconced in a Me/Mine entitlement culture of whiners and malcontents. It's frankly embarrassing because this unproductive noise is coming from the parents. And the kids are watching. Yeah, GenX, we are that old.

GenX? We knew it wasn't about us. The adults didn't even know we were around, generally. Left to our own devices, we made our own fun. Any parent paying attention at the time would agree. Kids with a purpose of their own design are brilliant and unstoppable and totally fun to watch. Doesn't matter what corner of the globe they hail from; kids are dynamos capable of miracles and made of rubber. We made minibikes from literal scrap and outfitted them with lawnmower engines. Then we built ramps and jumped our buddies or ran them into a tree at 30 mph. Usually both.

If we are not directing that energy with forethought, respect, and kindness towards the positive and productive, we are doing a gross disservice to the next generation. We need them to know their life is a project that requires learning and rewards responsibility. You want to live well? Learn, work and create that life. What do you want to be remembered for, complaining?

If our kids don't have an idea of how an adult behaves, how can they be expected to grow the eff up? The information below requires work and commitment and social skills and responsibility. All of which are in precious short supply today. The small shit is falling apart, and the big shit seems to be following.

I wanted my boys to get a nitro-boost of stuff they need know but no one would tell them. That's the reason Vito Corlcon, a 350lb drag queen and a goat all had to appear in the same letter like the Ghost Busters crossing plasma streams.

"Then it's easy to believe
Somebody's been lying to me
But when the wrong word goes in the right ear
I know why you've been lying to me
It's getting rough, off the cuff I've got to say enough's enough."

One Thing Leads to Another - The Fixx, Live in Concert, 1982

*Late November 202**

Hey There Charlie,

We're in the home stretch of 202. Crazy year, a lot of momentous doings. You, nailing work, getting paid, owning a home, travelling around, meeting new people, keeping in touch with your core homies, staying in awesome shape, building your crib around you in comfort and luxury.*

You got the game wired right now. Your foundation is rock solid. Now's the time to explore what keeps you happy and grounded. There's no clock ticking, no giant deadlines looming, no tests. Just life. That's a very freeing circumstance. Take your time in outfitting your house just the way you want it. Work your projects. Delegate. Stay high-profile to those who matter in your career. Continue your history of being smart, in control and in charge. It's got you this far, this fast.

Here's some hard-won advice from the old skunk:

- *Don't compare yourself to others. Why? Because we don't know. We don't know what their work involves. We don't know if they have to blow their boss for a raise. We don't know what they're struggling with at home, internally, at work. Everybody has a backstory we're not privy to. Be nice. Be helpful. Be professional. Be there. But don't fall into the "Them vs Me" trap. You can't win that game.*

- *If you make the rules, you can't lose. If you own the process, create the structure, make it work, others buy in, you move ahead. On your terms.*

- *Sweat the small stuff. Everybody will tell you the opposite but that's bullshit. In life, you have very little control. However, there are things you can control. You can control your actions, your reactions, your spending, your schedule, your relationships, and a host of other stuff.*
- *It's the small stuff that marks you as a person of note. It's the small stuff that creates your public and internal persona. Sweat being on time. Sweat being prepared. Sweat being present and engaged in personal interactions. Sweat listening and understanding what the other person is saying. Sweat your personal appearance. Sweat the quality of your work. Sweat staying on the good side of the law. Sweat deadlines. All small stuff, all within your control.*
- *If the small shit falls apart, the big shit goes too.*
- *Maintenance is key. Maintenance of your stuff is a never-ending series of tiny jobs that allow you to avoid giant, shitty, expensive jobs.*
- *Wipe down your bathroom a couple times a week with a Clorox wipe. It takes 2 minutes literally. You'll never have to power-wash a piss and toothpaste and soap scum encrusted abomination. Your bathroom will be good for unexpected guests.*
- *Maintain your car. Oil, tires, inspection. Address mechanical problems while they're still small and less expensive. This goes for your house too. Pick small projects in your house and chip away at them.*
- *Maintain yourself. Maintain your wardrobe. Exercise, decent food, plenty of sleep, meaningful work, meaningful relationships, meaningful fun, plenty of down-time to relax and regroup.*
- *If you are good, your stuff stays good. In fact, just knowing you have your maintenance under control will give you a nice measure of mental comfort. It'll guide your spending. It'll guide your saving. It'll guide your schedule.*

It's called "Having your shit wired tight".

Anyway, there's a few things to consider on a gray, last day of November in Wuhan Times. Git yourself a snow shovel.

Be good.
Love,
Dad
*November, 202**

Ahoy the Charlie,

Nothing like getting lashed by rain for a week. It's awesome. We needed the wet, we needed the cool, we needed the streets cleaned. Sucks for running though. I hope you have a hat or pinny or something visible and reflective now that night is coming earlier and earlier. Can't run a 1/2 marathon if you're laid up in the hospital. Can't collect a paycheck either.

Stay safe and reflected and lit up on the streets.

How about them Phils getting a playoff slot? They look pretty good. Nola finally producing. Fall ball. It's good stuff.

Anyway, it was good talking to you. Here are my thoughts:

Don't sweat your company hiring some higher positions over you. It happens. It happens often. It's not gonna stop happening.

The best thing you can do is be productive with your projects, mentoring to your underlings, helpful to your co-workers and insightful, available and enthusiastic to your superiors. That's where the rubber meets the road. That's where you create your work identity and reputation. That's where money, respect and opportunity come from.

Starting fresh somewhere means 3x the assache, proving yourself all over again and zero flexibility because you are an unknown. The extra money is a thin prize.

When genuinely solid opportunities present themselves, you'll know. Your longevity at this company and reputation for excellence can get you a new job very quickly. But despite the money, you will be starting as the noob with way more unknowns than knowns about what and who you just joined. Be smart, be picky, be the driver, not the desperate schlub.

Understanding the market for your skill set, the players in the market, the good and the shit companies, the solid projects and hot topics are an on-going part of your job. Keep learning and exploring and proffering recommendations to the bosses. That's the real job search activity that will pay in the future. Trust me on that one.

You've already shown an exceptional ability to quickly create a rapport with people. You can thank me for that. If a headhunter can't create a rapport in 3 minutes, he better find a new gig. Anyway, your ability with people will make them remember you. It will grease work for a smoother flow. It will create that reputation of a confident executioner. It'll get you noticed and sought after.

Get your LinkedIn stuffed with recommendations. Make that a side project. A proper LinkedIn recommendation list will have them coming after you.

So......Happy Autumn! You've got it wired. Do your thang.

Love,
Dad

Bet you never saw the word 'weather' repeated four times in one sentence before.

*August, 202**

Hiya my Charlie,

Not even September yet and the leaves are starting to go. We had a weird, wet summer with a couple hot weeks. Just like we had a weird, wet winter with a couple cold weeks. Looks like PA weather is heading towards Maryland weather and Maryland weather is heading toward Carolina weather.

As we're heading into colder months, it might be a good

time to dust off the home inspector's binder and see what you could chip away at. AC's will be going on sale. Gardening stuff will be going on sale. Make sure your emergency fund is topped off.

Home heater repairs and stuff tend to happen in the Fall.

Love seeing your travel plans. Yeah, work is work, but folding in fun time is crucial to keeping your sanity. Work will never go away. It's your attitude that makes it bearable or miserable.

It's the people you work with that make it fun or a challenge. Take your time and assemble a strong team with some fun or like-minded individuals and work is less of a chore and more like an essential part of your deal that delivers plusses to your bank account.

You are in the labor/production part of your career. You are building a network, refining your execution skills, developing a visible work ethic that other people will judge as effective or lacking. Fuck them.

Your network, your skills and your work ethic are the essential building blocks of your next steps. Not theirs.

Live within your means. Simple routines. Simple life. Simple problems.

Consider other people's motivations when you are interacting. Why? Because they don't give a dick about you or your story or your path.

People think about themselves. That's how the human animal do. Don't compare, don't invest personal angst, don't get swept up in bullshit that you don't own. Only pick fights when sitting out of the fight would negatively affect your dough and your flow. If it don't. Don't.

The time may come when you're sitting on the BOA (recruiting term: Balls Of your Ass), waiting for a new opportunity to materialize. If that happens, you'll be in ice-ball hell wondering how you're going to live. Avoid that. I'll say it again. Avoid that. You might not have any control over the future, but you do have control over the important stuff, like padding your emergency funds and keeping your eyes and ears open.

Set some small, attainable goals to better your health, better your mind, better your workplace, better your relationships. Keep that routine up and you'll be king of the world. Note, none of this cost money, yet they are the most important factors to a happy life.

Here's looking forward to the change of seasons. You've got a busy September coming up. It's gonna be great. Appreciate where you've gotten yourself. It's a good life. And, you made it.

Be good.
Love,
Dad

*October 201**

Hey There Mikey,

Happy partial snow day. Maybe a little extra time to get stuff done.....or sleep. :-D

So going to school, especially a military academy, is supposed to build character. But has anyone there approached what that actually means? I've always believed that character and personality are 2 different things.

Character, I think, is your inner guide, your personal set of beliefs, morals, way of thinking and reacting to situations. I think character is based on upbringing, mental ability, your personal code of conduct and interaction. It slowly grows with experience when we interact with others and witness character in action. It prompts how we manage circumstances. It's more objective than subjective.

In the scheme of life, character is much more important than personality. Why? Well, maybe because we get internal satisfaction, or stability, or big dough, or personal meaning from our character. It's how we do. Maybe it's based on goals, maybe it's based on keeping God happy, maybe it's based on basic human decency.

Regardless, character is unique to you. It is who you choose to be deep down. I believe it's learned and grown and personally tuned through the years. People recognize character. People who pay attention can see past personality to one's character. It's probably your most important possession. It's what makes The Mike, The Mike.

Personality, on the other hand is what you allow others to see. Personality can be the brand you create; athlete, student, aficionado, cable-free with awesome hair, Sack-Meister. It's the very subjective mix of your mental outlook, feelings and actions. It's interaction and behavior and choice. It moves and changes with the times. Your big brother has moved from athlete to hip-hop fan to frat-bro to investor to working man in his personality while keeping a stable, effective, nice guy character.

Personality makes you feel like you. Character makes you act like you.

Personality is the outer. Character is the inner.

In fresh relationships, people respond to the personality. As relationships develop, people come to recognize your character.

Character is getting up every day and doing your job. Personality is doing your job wearing funny socks.

For me, early character was defined by Catholic School. Be good, pray, go to church, do your homework, suffer through things and be quiet because you'll go to hell if you don't. As I grew up and away, character became a choice for me. Who do I need to be to be a successful human? What is my definition of success? Who do I need to be to provide for me and my family?

What deep traits do I need to cultivate to be a person of character?

Here's one snippet of my character that I've always tried

to adhere to: In The Godfather, Johnny Fontain meets with Vito Corleone in his office during the wedding. He starts yamming and whinging about some part he wants in a movie and how the producer won't let him get it and wah wah wah, what do I do? Vito slaps him hard in the face and yells "Be a man!" at him. That scene has always resonated with me.

When shit happens, and shit always happens, what do I do, how do I react? Hopefully I react like a god-damn man. Yeah, Vito fixes the problem, but Johnny has to go perform at the wedding with a scarlet hand-print on his face. Lesson learned.

So be conscious of your 'deep down'. What makes you happy, what are your immediate and distant goals, what gives the Mike personal satisfaction, what do you connect with, what drives your actions? Cultivate your character to suit those goals and create new goals.

Too many people nowadays are purely driven by personality. Look at me! I'm twerking! I'm a dude in a dress! My hair is pink! I tattooed my face! I'm taking a goat to prom! Their self-worth is measured by how people react to them. That's very sad and superficial. It's also a losing game because it's all been done before and as we know, people generally don't give a dick about you or your story or your path. So why stress?

It's also straight-up bullshit. It's your character that makes you a person of distinction, not yer bow-tie and leggings.

I don't give a balz if you're dressed in a 3-piece suit and make a zillion dollars. If I tell you something in confidence and the next day 10 people know about it. You are not a person of character. You're a pedestrian shit-bag and of no use to me.

You could be a 350lb drag-queen but if you give your seat to an old lady on the train, or help a kid with their algebra homework, you likely have something to offer the world.

Stay Strong.
Love,
Dad

Once upon a time, Charlie had a Biochemistry teacher fresh out of school who failed everybody. Her class created an issue of some summer credits or some more summer credits for graduation. If it went bad, he was dead set on taking her class again to prove a point. Instead of telling him to go kick her ass, he deserved some honest answers.

*April, 201**

Hiya Charlie,

Letter number Heinz 57.
Happy last day of April, the worst month of the year. Nothing good ever happens in April. It's wet, gross, sneezy and weird. It was great to see you this weekend. It was a very nice couple of days. Love seeing you and your brudder together.
Don't let this 3 or 6 credit thing bother you too much. It's bullshit. Why? It's the difference between a pain in the balz and a pain in the balz. Either way you have some extra work to do. You do the work. You get out. Tomorrow's May. Good things happen in May. If my Voodoo incantations and rain dance worked, you'll be seeing a 'C' tomorrow and just have a quick 3-week camp to do before you're home free. If not, it's OK. You do the 6 weeks of camp and skate. Why? Nobody fails a camp.
Playing the 'fuck-you' card and making that teacher look at your puss for 6 weeks on a re-try is not the move. There's no guarantee you pass. None. Plus, you potentially waste the summer and will have to find a new place to live. That's something you need to avoid at all costs.
So sit tight, burn some sage, say a prayer, kill a chicken,

light a candle, do an interpretive dance. I hope the 'C' comes through in the final grade. If it doesn't, call her, ask her 1) "Is this my final grade?" 2) "I know you were not accepting extra credit in our last correspondence, but are you accepting it now?"

Good Luck.

It will all work out in the end regardless of all your worries now. So be easy. It's not life or death. It's not even that important. The GPA is a total non-factor. Nobody but academics give a fuck about GPA because that's how they define their existence. Nobody in the business world gives a rat's nutsack about GPA.... or Academics for that matter.

Never let test scores hold you hostage. Life is not measured in A's, B's or C's anywhere but the defunct and corrupt, academic world. You've played that game like a pro for 4 years. Time to wrap it up and get into the world where life is measured by who you are and how you do. And you are rock solid and you certainly know how to do. Ask any executive in the world if they want a person who is good every day or great once in a while and they will opt for #1 every time. You're good all the time and usually outstanding.

So please, take it easy, it seems like a huge deal right now, but you will get through it and everything will be fine. Plan for the worst-case scenario and be happy if you catch a break.

Be good.
Love,
Dad

Any GenX Dad would've counselled the same and hence the boy graduated in 4 years with a Bachelors in Biology and a Bachelors in Business. Another testimony to grit.

And here below is a final structural building block you need to know but nobody will tell you. My GenX compatriots will agree because our veterans from 5 previous wars led us by example.

That and the fact that we were the last generation to use suntan oil instead of sunscreen.

    •Ya'll can't be soft.

We had a very popular saying back in the day. "Life's a Bitch and then you Die." I don't know its origin; I just know I've heard that phrase uttered at least once every year since I was old enough to listen. GenX heard, absorbed, and then happily went about our business. What we understood from practical experience was summed up by Marcus. **"Choose not to be harmed—and you won't feel harmed. Don't feel harmed—and you haven't been."**

**"It's my turn
To start from number one
Trying to undo
Some damage that's been done
But now it's my turn
To reach and touch the sky
No one's gonna say
At least I didn't try."**

It's My Turn – Diana Ross, To Love Again, 1981

Chapter 18
Police Briefs

What we don't know can hurt us. As GenX kids, we were constantly learning and observing things that would benefit us and things which would adversely affect us. From our largely ignored vantage points in shopping center parking lots, the Mall, the playgrounds, the bus downtown and a myriad of other places we probably oughtn't have been, we witnessed stupidity in action.

We came, we saw and we digested things like shoplifters getting cuffed, drunks getting rousted, illicit drug use and violence of all kinds. Hell, at my 10 Year Grade-School Reunion, we ran out of beer, the DJ got his nose broken and my man Sketties went home with our 4th Grade Math Teacher. The good stuff I can't even tell you about. Suffice it to say, GenX's roaming allowed us to witness and partake of the world in all its glory.

Fun was had and lessons were learned. Very little was ever documented.

Now today, I happen to live in the best place in the world. And our Local Police are not only awesome, but they truly represent GenX in action and humor and rock like no other. You'll see that in the transcriptions below. Our county police HQ routinely publishes weekly briefs and posts them on the neighborhood internet sites. They are quite outstanding. I've only changed locations and names, but the lessons are there and the presentation funny as nutz.

I figured sharing our local police briefs with the boys would not only be fun and a connection to home but might also provide real illustrations of stupid shit that will get you in trouble. Consider it an extra shot of what you need to know but nobody will tell you. I take no credit, all hail to the men and women of the Dept tasked with wrangling humanity on a daily basis, then being brave enough to lay it out to the community as hilarious cautionary tales.

It's also an affirmation that there are good people in the world committed to the betterment of the hive. And that's a great thing.

*January, 201**

Happy 1st Day of 2nd Semester my boyo!

Here's some news from home.

OLD TOWN POLICE DEPARTMENT BLOTTER

FROM 12/31/201 to 01/06/201* POLICE RESPONDED TO 119 CALLS FOR SERVICE INCLUDING 10 TRAFFIC ACCIDENTS. THE FOLLOWING IS A BRIEF SUMMARY OF NOTABLE INCIDENTS.*

On 12/31 at 1:21PM, police responded to Joe's supermarket parking lot for the report of a traffic altercation. The caller reported that a woman driving a VW almost hit him while she was backing out of a parking spot. As he was telling her about the close call, the woman took off and ran over his foot. The caller responded by throwing two 12 packs of soda at her car and denting the trunk of the VW.

On 12/31 at 2:45PM, a resident in the 400 block of Vanderslice Street reported that he came home from work and noticed that the rear window of his Honda Civic had been shattered. He looked inside the car and there was a golf ball on the back seat.

On 1/1 at 2:02AM, officers were downtown at closing time and a raucous crowd emptied out of Duke's Pub into the street. The group was yelling back and forth and two men were posturing like they were going to settle things with their fists. One of the men, a 23-year-old Newtown resident, continued to behave poorly after the officers dispersed the group so he was issued a summons for disorderly conduct.

On 1/1 at 2:13AM, police responded to an apartment in the unit block of Big Street for the report of a break-in. Officers located a 22-year-old Midtown man who was drunk and walked into the wrong apartment. He was looking for a friend's apartment and got confused. Understandably, the tenants were alarmed when the stranger walked in the back door. The man was arrested for public drunkenness and trespassing and released when he was sober.

On 1/1 at 2:41AM, police responded to the 100 block of Long Street for the report of a stalker. A group of women reported that a man was following them as they walked on the sidewalk. He was hissing at them and claimed to be the Messiah. Officers searched the area but could not locate the false prophet.

On 1/2 at 6:34PM, a resident in the 100 block of Wee Street reported that someone tried to sicken his dog by throwing chocolate and bacon grease into his fenced backyard.

On 1/2 at 7:07PM, police responded to the 100 block of Lang Street for a parking dispute. The caller reported that the driver of a Ford pick-up parked in his driveway and when he told him to move, the guy cursed him out and punched him in the face. The aggressor left before the police arrived but Officer King was able to identify him. The 26-year-old Lowtown man will be receiving a summons for harassment.

On 1/3 at 9:28AM, police responded to the intersection of Loe Street and Hai Street for the report of a car crash involving a pedestrian. A 63-year-old Oldtown man was hit by a Benz being driven by a 77-year-old Newtown woman. Several people witnessed the crash and police obtained video footage from a nearby business. The pedestrian was taken to Sidetown Hospital for treatment by Oldtown Ambulance.

On 1/4 at 11:13PM, a resident in the 100 block of Side Street reported that she heard a loud thud on her front porch. She looked outside and saw a man lying face down on the porch and he appeared to be passed out. Officers arrived and could not revive the man so an ambulance responded to take him to the hospital for an alcohol overdose. The 27-year-old Oldtown man was issued a summons for public drunkenness.

On 1/5 at 3:15AM, Sgt. Bob noticed a man sitting in an alley in the 100 block of Long Street. The 21-year-old Oldtown man was highly intoxicated and could not function. He was arrested for public drunkenness and released to his sister at the police station.

On 1/5 at 1:33PM, police responded to the Ymart store for a missing person report. The caller reported that she got separated from her 57-year-old boyfriend inside the store and can't find him. Cpl. Klinger arrived and the boyfriend was sitting by the entrance waiting for her to finish shopping.

On 1/5 at 7:10PM, police responded to the bar at the Plum Tree Inn for the report of a disturbance. The bartender reported that a customer was using profanity and arguing with another patron. An officer spoke to the irate customer and he explained that he was upset because the other patron let his two dogs run loose on the outside patio and he is afraid of dogs. The bartender flagged the angry man and told him he was no longer welcome at the bar.

On 1/6 at 12:57AM, Officer King was on bike patrol in the 100 block of Long Street and noticed a barefoot man wandering around with no pants on. The man was wearing blue boxers and he was drunk and disoriented. The 56-year-old man told the officer that he lives on the north side of town and left his pants and shoes at home. He was taken to Sidetown Hospital by ambulance for an evaluation and was issued a summons for public drunkenness.

On 1/6 at 1:36AM, an officer was flagged down by an agitated man outside Duke's Pub. The man told the officer that he was just "attacked by a crazy man" inside the bar. Officers spoke to the bouncers at the bar and learned that the man was not attacked but he was flagged from the bar for vomiting on the floor.

On 1/6 at 2:23AM, Officer Bill observed a man peeing in the vestibule at the Oldtown Village Art Center in the 100 block of Long Street. The 29-year-old Sidetown man was issued a summons for disorderly conduct.

On 1/6 at 5:18PM, police responded to the 100 block of S. West Street for the report of a woman walking around wearing nothing but a trench coat. Cpl. Klinger located the woman in the parking lot of the laundromat and she was dressed in only a duster and the temperature was 43 degrees. The 32-year-old woman appeared to be suffering from a mental health condition so she was taken to Sidetown Hospital for an evaluation.

On 1/6 at 7:50PM, a resident reported that she could hear a woman screaming in the 100 block of North Street. The resident called back and cancelled- she explained that her neighbor was just excited because Parkey shanked the field goal and the Eagles beat the Bears. Go Birds!

Talk to you soon. Good Luck!

Stay Strong.
Love,
Dad

*February, 201**

Hiya Mike,

3 more weeks to go. Hang tough. Hope you are doing well. You looked great on the Sunday call. Here's the police briefs for Oldtown last week. Your school made it in.

OLDTOWN POLICE DEPARTMENT BLOTTER

FROM 02/11/201 to 02/17/201* POLICE RESPONDED TO 109 CALLS FOR SERVICE INCLUDING 16 TRAFFIC ACCIDENTS. THE FOLLOWING IS A BRIEF SUMMARY OF NOTABLE INCIDENTS.*

On 2/11 at 4:11PM, a resident of the Creek Crossing apartments reported that someone entered her unlocked Hyundai Santa Fe overnight and stole $70 from her wallet.

On 2/12 at 2:10PM, police responded to the unit block of E. Hai Street for the report of a neighbor dispute. A group of neighbors were arguing with each other about snow displacement etiquette. The group agreed to shovel their snow in a peaceful manner.

On 2/12 at 9:19PM, a resident in the 500 block of Wilson Street reported that a person dressed in all black clothing was pulling the door handles on several cars on her street. Officers checked the area and tracked a set of footprints in the snow but they did not lead to the prowler.

On 2/13 at 7:20PM, police responded to the 100 block of Long Street for the report of a homeless man loitering in several businesses. The 43-year-old man was given several warnings to leave Duke's Pub but he refused so he was escorted outside and issued a summons for trespassing. He told the officers that he was cold and hungry and could not get into a shelter. Officer Bob gave the man $10 to buy dinner and then gave him a ride to his cousin's house in Westtown.

On 2/15 at 11:59AM, police received information that a wanted woman would be coming to the Oldtown School that afternoon. Officers waited in the main office and arrested Susan Kate age 25 of Newtown when she arrived. Kate had two County bench warrants and a Domestic Relations warrant. Adding insult to injury, Kate had some weed on her when she was picked up so she faces additional drug charges. Kate was turned over to Newtown PD.

On 2/15 at 3:15PM, a resident in the 100 block of Short Street reported that someone damaged her Jeep Wrangler by beating on it with a blunt object. The owner suspects that an ex-boyfriend caused the damage.

On 2/15 at 7:22PM, police responded to an apartment in the 100 block of Box Street for the report of a noise complaint. The caller reported that his upstairs neighbor makes excessive noise on a regular basis. Officers advised the caller to file a complaint with his landlord. They were told that the guy making the noise is the landlord.

On 2/16 at 2:45AM, police responded to the Sunoco gas station on Rt. 66 for the report of a disturbance. A person who uses a wheelchair reported that the driver of a white sedan almost ran him over in the parking lot. Officers spoke to the night clerk and learned that the man had been loitering around the store since 11PM and refused to leave the property when asked. Officer Bill ran a check on the 50-year-old homeless man and learned that he had a County bench warrant. Joe Bob was arrested and taken to the county jail in Sidetown.

On 2/16 at 9:45PM, police responded to Pacos Pizza in the 100 block of Long Street for the report of an intoxicated person inside the restaurant. An employee reported that a woman walked into the pizzeria, threw up all over the floor, and walked out. Officers located the 36-year-old Oldtown woman nearby and issued her a summons for public drunkenness. The woman's friend agreed to drive her home to her husband.

On 2/17 at 2:15AM, police responded to the 100 block of Loe Street for the report of a drunken man sitting in the middle of the road. Officers checked the area and located the man staggering near the Oldtown River Trail entrance on Quiet Road. The caller was trying to keep the man from walking into traffic. The 28-year-old Newtown resident could not provide his address or form a sentence. He was arrested for public drunkenness and released when he was sober.

I'm glad we were not in Pacos eating a pie when that lady walked in. Sheesh, that's some nads.

Stay strong.
Love,
Dad

March, 201*

Hiya Charlie,

Be sure to check out the supermoon tonight.
   Here's the Police Briefs from Paddy's Day Weekend.

OLDTOWN POLICE DEPARTMENT BLOTTER (St. Patrick's Day Weekend Edition)

FROM 03/14/201 to 03/17/201* POLICE RESPONDED TO 79 CALLS FOR SERVICE INCLUDING 5 TRAFFIC ACCIDENTS. THE FOLLOWING IS A BRIEF SUMMARY OF NOTABLE INCIDENTS.*

On 3/14 at 1:24PM, a resident in the Oldtown Village apartment complex called the police because he could not get his motorized wheelchair started. Officer Bill looked under the hood and was able to restore power to the wheelchair.

On 3/14 at 11:05PM, police responded to an apartment in the RiverTrail community for a harassment complaint. The caller reported that her ex-boyfriend was circling her apartment building in his pick-up truck trying to get her attention. Officer Andy stopped the ex and issued him a warning about the harassment and trespassing.

On 3/15 at 1:25AM, police responded to the 100 block of West Street for the report of a suspicious person. The caller reported that a man dressed in a bathrobe was running around the parking lot jumping on cars. Officers located the man and he was actually wearing pajama pants and no shirt. He told the officers that he was training for a Tough Mudder race and promised to stay off of people's cars. None of the cars appeared to be damaged.

On 3/16 at 12:28PM, police responded to the RiverTrail neighborhood for the report of a hazardous condition. The caller reported that a group of teenagers were car surfing on a Ford sedan. Officer Wendy located the teens and explained the perils of standing on moving cars.

On 3/16 at 9:00PM, officers saw a man walking downtown

drinking a cocktail and asked him to pour it out. He was given a warning and sent on his way. Fifteen minutes later, the man reappeared with another cocktail in his hand. The 50-year-old Oldtown man was issued a summons for the open container ordinance. Long Street is not Bourbon Street.

On 3/16 at 10:05PM, police responded to the 100 block of Long Street for the report of an assault with injuries. Officers encountered a woman with a split lip and chipped tooth and learned that her husband shoved her and she fell face first onto the sidewalk. The husband approached the officers and admitted that he just pushed his wife to the ground. The 49-year-old Newtown man was arrested for assault and public drunkenness.

On 3/16 at 10:53PM, a resident in the RiverTrail community reported that the driver of a red Jeep hit a tree on Rt. 66 and drove off with a flat tire. A short time later, Newtown PD located the Jeep limping along on the East County side and arrested the 44-year-old Newtown man for DUI.

On 3/16 at 11:15PM, Officer Bill was on bike patrol downtown and noticed a man relieving himself on the Side Street sidewalk. The 34-year-old man from Way Out of Town, was issued a summons for the public urination ordinance.

On 3/16 at 11:58PM, police responded to the area of Brown Street and Green Avenue to check on the welfare of a pedestrian who was staggering and falling on the sidewalk. Officers located the man and he was bleeding badly from his forehead and could not function. The 28-year-old Newtown man was taken to the hospital by ambulance and issued a summons for public drunkenness.

On 3/17 at 2:20AM, a bar patron approached Cpl. Klinger outside Liam's Pub and reported that a woman took his cell phone from him inside the bar. The officer investigated and learned that the woman took the man's cell phone because she caught him taking photos of her over the top of the stall in the woman's restroom. The officer checked the phone and confirmed that there were nude photos of the woman taken over the stall. The 43-year-old peeping tom from Newtown was charged with invasion of privacy and his phone was confiscated.

On 3/17 at 3:00AM, an Twp. PD officer stopped the driver of a Mercedes SUV near the Side Street Bridge because the car had a flat tire and was being driven on the rim. The driver told the officer that he may have hit something in Oldtown but wasn't sure.

On 3/17 at 7:25PM, Officer Bob was on bike patrol near the town center and heard a crash coming from the area of Side Street. The officer saw an orange Toyota Prius speeding away so he pulled the driver over. The officer confirmed that the driver just hit a parked car and she appeared to be under the influence, Sally Anne age 21 of Northtown, failed field sobriety tests and was arrested for DUI.

Be good.
Love,
Dad

And finally, the one where Mike had a tooth knocked out by an overly aggressive pull-up bar. I laughed out loud reading this one again. It's the GenX version of "Rub some dirt on it."

*May, 201**

Hiya Mikey,

Tough luck with your toof. I'm telling you, they will cement

it back in at the dentist. If you need a good temporary fix, use a dab of superglue. It'll hold it in place until you get to the dentist. You got a bunch of other toofus working for you. It'll be fine.

Here's some police briefs to keep you entertained in the meantime.

OLDTOWN POLICE DEPARTMENT BLOTTER

FROM 05/20/201 to 05/26/201* POLICE RESPONDED TO 141 CALLS FOR SERVICE INCLUDING 10 TRAFFIC ACCIDENTS. THE FOLLOWING IS A BRIEF SUMMARY OF NOTABLE INCIDENTS.*

On 5/20 at 8:05PM, a resident in the 100 block of 2nd Avenue reported that two bulldog statues valued at $30 each were stolen from her front lawn.

On 5/21 at 2:02AM, police responded to the bar at the Old Creek Inn for the report of a disturbance involving a patron who was trying to make a cocaine deal inside the establishment. The man fled before the police arrived but officers located him a short time later at the 7-11 store. While the officers were talking to the intoxicated man, he indiscreetly tossed a packet of white powder on the ground. Tim Tiny, 37 of Oldtown, was arrested for the drug violation and public drunkenness.

On 5/21 at 11:08PM, police responded to a home in the unit block of High Street for the report of two suspicious men in the area. Officers encountered two men sitting in a gold Chevy with New Jersey tags- but the car smelled like it was from Colorado. The pair had been smoking marijuana and one of the men, Andrew Young 18 of Westtown, had a bag of weed stashed in his underpants so he was arrested and charged with the drug violation.

On 5/22 at 8:46PM, police responded to a home in the 200 block of Buchanan Street for the report of a disturbance. Officers spoke to a 54-year-old woman who explained that she was just yelling at her husband and everything was fine.

On 5/24 at 11:45AM, police responded to the ER at Sidetown Hospital for the report of a person taking wheelchairs without authorization. The 36-year-old woman told Officer Bob that she has been using the hospital wheelchairs for over a year to get back and forth from her house on Blythe Street. The officer informed her she cannot borrow medical equipment without permission.

On 5/24 at 12:00PM, police responded to Oldtown Federal Bank for the report of a woman trying to cash a fake paycheck. Betty Bounce, 19 of Royersford, was arrested and charged with forgery and bad checks. The woman's "employer" never heard of her.

On 5/25 at 1:50AM, police responded to the area of Long Street and Back Alley for the report of a shoeless man running in the middle of the road. Officers located the 21-year-old Newtown man who was drunk and clearly a danger to himself. He was arrested for public drunkenness and released when he was sober.

On 5/26 at 12:29AM, a 33-year-old Oldtown woman called the police to report that she wanted to come clean on a theft she committed in Virginia 15 years ago. She was referred to the local police in Virginia where the crime was committed.

On 5/26 at 1:20AM, police responded to Liam's Pub for the report of a patron passed out on the floor. The 25-year-old Newtown woman was taken to Sidetown Hospital by ambulance for an alcohol overdose and she was issued a summons for public drunkenness. Her boyfriend, 26 of

Newtown, was also drunk so he was flagged from the bar and left. Not to be deterred- he returned 15 minutes later and he was arrested for public drunkenness/disorderly conduct and was released when he was sober.

On 5/26 at 1:52AM, police were patrolling downtown and saw a large crowd lingering in front of Duke's Pub at closing time. Two women in the group were drunk and being aggressive toward each other. The women, ages 25 and 28 were given several opportunities to leave the area but they chose the alternative. They were both arrested for public drunkenness and disorderly conduct. One lady tried to kick an officer so she was charged with additional counts of assault and resisting arrest.

On 5/26 at 11:48PM, a couple flagged down Officer Bob and asked for a ride across town because they both had too much to drink. The officer gave them a courtesy ride home.

Enjoy your down-time and graduation practice.
  Tell the dentist you want a gold tooth.

Stay strong.
Love,
Dad

Please allow a slight detour into real, witnessed Americana. Our town sits at the frayed end of the American Rust Belt. A once bustling riverside community surrounding a prolific and internationally renowned steel mill that opened in 1790 and closed in the mid-1970's. The town fell on several decades of 1930's-style hard times during the GenX days. As suburban sprawl organically metastasized, our town was rediscovered and slowly revitalized. We moved here at the turn of this century and it retains a blue-collar, stoic and calloused demeanor while the new breweries, pubs, music venues and eateries are visited by folks from all neighboring areas.

Once upon a time the hardened population of this little town literally cooked themselves to a crisp to supply the world with the materials necessary to create infrastructure, modern industry and serious tools that won wars both civil and global. Now we're a resort for folks who obviously never read The Rules of Drinking. That our town is bustling again is no secret. It created the environment that created our tremendous peacekeepers and their bulletins. Times change and GenX sits back and enjoys the show with a rueful smile and a cold beverage from our carefully cultivated vantage points. We're happy our Blue has things under control.

So, if you are here in the US or in my town or at my front door and dead set on making trouble, please realize, that makes you The Opposition.

We have heroes in place to stop you outright or gently steer you in the correct direction. Your actions will dictate the result. Read that again.

**"One way or another I'm gonna find ya.
I'm gonna getcha getcha getcha getcha."**

One Way or Another– Blondie, Parallel Lines, 1978

Chapter 19
The Code

This entire exercise of writing to my boys had been organically pushing towards this point. The life lessons, the wisdom of the ages, the prompts, the parables, the warnings, the praise, were more about fun than education and really just a selfish effort to maintain a positive link with my children who I missed. In the same breath I hoped I had given them some practical information and true-life lessons from not one school of thought but many schools of thought through history.

I hoped I had given them a broad enough spectrum of worldly experience that they could pick and choose a set of values that they could apply and practice today, out in the world, to their advantage and to others' benefit. If this sounds suspiciously like a Code to live by, you nailed it.

GenX had many Codes of Conduct. We had the Playground Code, the Schoolyard Code, Basketball Court Code. These codes defined the etiquette of interaction, turn-taking, new kids, disputes, team choosing, what have you. We had the Code of Church, The Code of Maneuvering in a Packed School Hallway, The I Call Shotgun Code, The Gimme Your Keys Code. We knew how to act appropriately in those situations. We were essentially self-governed.

A guy in the back wants an example of what's in the Church Code.

Off the top of my head, sir. "Don't fart at a funeral."
Next.

*Summer, 201**

Happy Wednesday Cholly!

That was an excellent text you sent yesterday. How cool is it to find odd stuff at random that few people ever get to see? A Hellbender? Who even knows what that is? Except us who gave you guys a rubber one to play with when you were little. I'm glad you are getting to do some cool stuff this summer. I hope your presentations, paper and tests go very well and you get out of there quickly, easily, degreed and unscathed.

Me and mom and the doogan are basically hanging out. It's hot. We're working. Doogan's shooting out giant wads of fuzz.

So, now you're just about done with school. It'll give you some time to consider things. Here's a couple things to think about.

Understand your own personal moral compass.

Me and Mom and most people from our demographic and generation were driven hard by our Irish-Catholic, working-class parents. Some carry that mind-set on with 1950's fervor. Me and Mom didn't. For a number of reasons.

What we did try to do was instill in you the importance of treating people with kindness and fairness.

Religion is a job; doing what Jesus/Yoda/Oprah/Yahweh/ Buddah tells you to do and paying the man. A job is a job; doing what the boss tells you to do and making sure the man gets paid. Being a kid and a student is a job; doing what your parents and teachers tell you to do and paying your dues.

It's time for you to decide, deep down, who exactly you want to be. Your personal moral compass should be your own, private belief system. Nothing dictated by circumstances or others, just a code that fits how you treat others and how you expect others to treat you. The Duke might've said it best. It's simple, but right the fuck on.

"I won't be wronged. I won't be insulted. I won't be laid a-hand on. I don't do these things to other people, and I require the same from them."

— John Wayne "The Shootist"

I'm happy that you are a person who is very strong, very kind, very fair, very gracious and smart enough to know truth from bullshit. You're not a sheep. If that's the best me and Mom could do for you. It's pretty goddamn good.

If your values match your strengths and your strengths match your career you will have an easier ride than most.

If who you are is aligned with what you believe and what you do, you are way ahead of the game. People don't tend to think that way. People tend do what they're told. You are the captain now. Decide who you are. Decide what you're best at. Decide what you want to do. Decide how you'd like things to play out in the long run.

Your values and strengths may evolve over time. Your core moral compass will likely stay pretty consistent.

Be centered but check your alignment from time to time. There's countless paths, decisions and recalculations in your future. Know yourself. Again, The Duke.
"Tomorrow is the most important thing in life. Comes into us at midnight very clean. It's perfect when it arrives and it puts itself in our hands. It hopes we've learned something from yesterday."
- John Wayne

Have a great day my bud. These are exciting and weird times but you continue to be the boss.

Be good.
Love
  Dad

*May, 202**

Happy Birthday Month Mike,

Finally on the tail-end of a cold, wet Sprang. Right now it's sunny but 53 degrees and cold as balz in the house. The new windows do a great job holding in the heat. They also hold in the cold. The heat's set at 59 degrees. I may have to remedy that while my fingers still work.

I took the doogan around early this morning and she told me it was cold, then pinched off a quick dump and 5 whizzes and ran back to her bed. She just whoofed at me and probably wants to go out now that the sun's shining and we're pushing lunchtime.

So today you're gonna hear my take on The Code.

Here's the deal, Religion as a social institution is failing as the older generations are kicking off and the younger generations see them as the faulty, money-making schemes that they are. Religions, for all their man-made problems and issues, provided people with a Code. The Golden Rule, treat others like you would be treated, no swearing, stealing, killing, banging the neighbor's wife.

The newer religions don't necessarily carry any more or less wisdom than the older ones. Jews, for example, shouldn't steal, worship idols or eat meat cut off a living animal. Buddhism can be distilled down to "Don't kill, steal, commit adultery, lie or use intoxicants. The Hindus believe gods and goddesses can be spirits, trees, and animals. Personally, I love this point of view.

This year, The Catholic Church created a special dispensation for Paddy's Day in the US. Since 3/17 fell on a meatless Friday during Lent, it was OK, just this once, for Catholics in the US to eat meat without going to hell. Look it up. I guess the Catholics in Ireland missed out on their corned beef and cabbage. I'd be pissed.

There are other Codes:

John Wayne's Code
- *Look out for your own.*
- *Always help someone in need.*
- *Finish what you start.*
- *Know where to draw the line.*
- *Never bother another man's horse.*
- *Talk less, say more.*
- *If you make a promise, keep it.*
- *Be tough but fair.*
- *Honesty is absolute.*
- *I won't be wronged. I won't be insulted. I won't be laid a-hand on. I don't do these things to other people, and I require the same from them.*

Steve Jobs Code
- *Simplicity, innovation, and perfectionism.*

Ben Franklin's Code:
- *TEMPERANCE. Eat not to dullness; drink not to elevation.*
- *SILENCE. Speak not but what may benefit others or yourself; avoid trifling conversation.*
- *ORDER. Let all your things have their places; let each part of your business have its time.*
- *RESOLUTION. Resolve to perform what you ought; perform without fail what you resolve.*
- *FRUGALITY. Make no expense but to do good to others or yourself; i.e., waste nothing.*
- *INDUSTRY. Lose no time; be always employ'd in something useful; cut off all unnecessary actions.*
- *SINCERITY. Use no hurtful deceit; think innocently and justly, and, if you speak, speak accordingly.*
- *JUSTICE. Wrong none by doing injuries, or omitting the benefits that are your duty.*
- *MODERATION. Avoid extremes; forbear resenting injuries so much as you think they deserve.*

- *CLEANLINESS. Tolerate no uncleanliness in body, clothes, or habitation.*
- *TRANQUILLITY. Be not disturbed at trifles, or at accidents common or unavoidable.*
- *CHASTITY. Rarely use venery but for health or offspring, never to dullness, weakness, or the injury of your own or another's peace or reputation.*
- *HUMILITY. Imitate Jesus and Socrates.*

Confucius' Code:
- *Respect*
- *Loyalty*
- *Hard Work*
- *Politeness*
- *Generosity*

Ghandi's Code:
- *Truth, non-violence, harmony, morality and simplicity*

As modern-day citizens, we see values such as respect, loyalty, industry, silence, honesty and humility to be in seriously short supply. Simple decency, simple respect, politeness, helpfulness seems to be non-existent. Angst, killing, entitlement, fear, mistrust and sloth are what is driving the US and most of the world these days.

How far we've come from the generations who built our country as a beacon of hope from wars, purges, famine, and strife. Those folks saw real, honest to shit hard times and rebuilt their lives here. Lives built pretty much on Confucius's platform of respect, loyalty, hard work, politeness, and generosity.

Today's population needs to drastically change their focus from internal to external. By internal, I'm looking at all the misery-trapped people who need a 'Safe Space' to function. Need their personal debts paid by others. Need a bully, a misogynist, government parasites, the weather, foreign warmongers, the stock market, lake-effect snow, evil wizards or pot-holes in the road to blame for their bad choices, laziness or inability to produce.

Complaints and bullshit, anger and angst fade to the background when you are too busy creating a life, family and community based on respect, hard work and loyalty. A real citizen can't afford to be a common dingus. See the external focus here?

It's easy to be alone and sad. In fact, it doesn't take any work at all to be a victim.

It takes work to be a productive citizen. That's the American Rub. If you do not have the internal attitude or motivation to create your life on your own merits why by Jebus would you ever expect someone to give you theirs?

If you focus on your job, your family, your skills, your neighbors, your community, your civic responsibilities, you will find the good things that define the US. Focus on the external in order to feed your self-worth.

I didn't raise my boys to be victims, sad do-nuthins or mean-spirited dicks. I raised you guys to be nice, smart, happy and helpful.

I've never really put together a personal Code for myself.

My life has been an exercise in attempting not to disappoint people. The parent, the priest, the teacher, the cops, the tax guy, the boss, the spouse, the kids. That's definitely an externally focused way of doing business, but it's stupid. The bar isn't only set low, the bar itself is all wrong. It doesn't factor in peace. it doesn't provide an ounce of self-worth. There's never a win or an end or a pause to reflect. Life's only the attempt to avoid the inevitable smack or punishment or disapproval when you fall short.

I will be creating a personal Code. If only to avoid the damaging mind-sets that were endemic to my generation of hard-working lapsed Catholics. It would be a very good exercise for you to formulate your own Code of Living. A list of bullets that you personally ascribe to. A series of reminders that keep you focused on the positive, productive and helpful. Think about it. I'd like to compare notes this summer in Scotland. I am giving this assignment to Mom and Charlie too.

Stay Strong,
Love,
Dad

This was the beginning of a very interesting project. The lovely and elusive Autumn my wife wanted in. The boys were interested in the exercise. We all had a few weeks to put our thoughts together before we met as a whole family again in the UK and compared Codes.

Now don't get excited. People's Codes are People's Codes. The resulting personal guidelines to life my family constructed for themselves are just that and not to be bandied about. Suffice it to say, we had hours of boisterous conversation as codes were presented and toasted and roasted. The insight, brevity, humor was remarkable and personal and thus needs to be respected.

However. Some of their stuff needs to appear simply because it's good advice and as real as real can be.

The points I will share below are completely randomized and probably direct excerpts of my family's personal Codes but need not be admitted to:

- Quality outweighs quantity.
- Slay the dragon, take the gold.
- You cannot always assume positive intent in others but always strive to have it yourself.
- Treat everything seriously but take nothing seriously.
- Live in the present, most of the time.
- Roll up your sleeves and get shit done.
- Treat everyone with respect, but only truly respect those who have earned it.

- Some people just blow mondo roo.
- Play is as important as work.
- Take risks. Don't feel compelled to stay on a linear path, it's ok to detour.
- Maximize your actions. Temper your reactions.
- Live fast, die old.

You've got around 165 years of living experience right there. The gist? "Yeah, people suck, go do something constructive anyway."

And if that's not a distillation of GenX ethos, I'll hang up my shillelagh.

Personal Codes. It's an interesting concept since people tend to do follow whoever's the noisiest these days. GenX was required to think for themselves and only trust what they knew to be true. Let's not let that novel concept die. I encourage you to create your own code and let your character rip. If for nuthin else, just to spite The Man.

"I sit by and watch the river flow,
I sit by and watch the traffic go.
Imagine something of your very own,
Something you can have and hold."

Dreaming – Blondie, Eat to the Beat, 1979

Chapter 20
Why's and a Couple How's

I'm sure you have some questions. The Why's and How's we've gleaned so far may point you in the right direction. Consider it a Magic 8-Ball with 20-some sides.

- Why? Post-Depression Era Moms. That's why.
- Why? Men. That's why. Who trusts a chatterbox?
- Why? Because being a man today is the same as being a man 1000 years ago despite what the media portrays.
- Why? Boys. That's why. Read to the end if you're considering getting one of your own.
- Why? Because the lovely and elusive Autumn my wife is a GenX female.
- Why? Because you would need 4 guys, a forklift and a panel truck to make your getaway.
- How? They probably issued a handbook.
- Why? GenX Females. That's why. Back away slowly and don't show fear.
- Why? It's a tough thing to bounce around a freshly empty house.
- Why? Because writing letters is personal.
- Why? Because people are people, were people, will be people and will build and burn as people have always done.
- Why? You gotta pay to play.
- Why? Boys. That's why. What's real fun without some risk?
- Why? They know we see through their rapidly

cooling bowel movement of self-serving policies and broken messages.

- Why? It's the difference between a pain in the balz and a pain in the balz.
- How do they manage that? By being scarier.
- Why? Boys. That's why. They should come with fine print. But they don't.
- Why? Miracles and such notwithstanding, childbirth is a dirty, nasty, hurtful bitch.
- Why? Boys. That's why. Make sure your insurance is paid up.
- Why? GenX women. Don't expect nonsense.
- Why? Because boys eat. They eat a bunch, and they eat often.
- Why? Because you can't reach every spot that needs attention by yourself.
- Why? Because you are funny, playful, caring, and protective.
- Why? Because today everybody has artificial access to everybody and real access to nobody.
- Why? Because GenX paid for this information in blood and bone and brain matter.
- Why? Because men and shiny stuff. That's why.
- Why? I think it's fucking funny.

"They tried to tame you, looks like they'll try again.
Wild boys never lose it,
Wild boys never chose this way,
Wild boys never close your eyes,
Wild boys always shine."

The Wild Boys – Duran Duran, Arena, 1984

Chapter 21
Talking Points

Let's take a quick look into the future. My boys had had the benefit of years to distill all the questionable information I've hosed you down with in the previous chapters. There are a lot of things for a parent to consider. There are topics that will spark necessary conversations.

If my boys retained a small percentage of what they deemed solid intel, I'd be happy. If this intel served to point them toward a smoother and potentially happier life, I'd have accomplished an important bit of fathering. Plus, I wouldn't have to haunt anybody out of spite.

If it made them laugh and strengthened our bonds and gave them insight into their stories and lineage, maybe they'd add their own chapters when their progeny graces the earth and continue the story. Hell, if nothing else, The Mayan Express might continue its Cannonball Run.

So here comes a final recap. Let's call them future talking points between you and your people. I'll call them:

My Code.

- **Number one. Fuck them.**
- **Hang in and trust the process.**
- **Check your alignment from time to time.**
- **It deserves our brains and efforts and best work.**
- **Are their goals in line with your goals?**
- **We should all hope for that brand of constancy and commitment.**
- **Relationships take work.**

- The risk exists, but the rewards are endless.
- Your treadmill is not mine to climb on.
- It's pretty easy to die.
- What matters is living the day you have in your grasp.
- No payment is required to get there.
- The alpha male knows how to cook.
- The rewards are never just monetary.
- Know when a change is gonna come.
- Ease some ease into your schedule.
- I'm opting for good.
- Ya'll can't think when it's too noisy.
- It will work out the way it is meant to work out.
- Honesty is never easy and fun.
- Life. It's a crapshoot that favors the prepared.
- It's called "Having your shit wired tight".
- Simple life. Simple problems.
- Character is getting up every day and doing your job.
- Ya'll can't be soft.
- Don't fart at a funeral.
- It doesn't take any work at all to be a victim.

"Would I lie to you?
Would I lie to you honey?
(Now honey would I lie to you?)
Now would I say something that wasn't true?
I'm asking you sugar,
Would I lie to you?"

Would I Lie to You? – The Eurythmics, Be Yourself Tonight, 1985

Chapter 22
Basta

Digging through the hundreds of letters I have written to my boys to date was fun and a bit crazy. Sounds like a big number but really translates to about 3 letters per kid per month since I started all those years ago. You've only seen a fraction. Still, the numbers do indicate a bit of Jiminy Cricket style obsession. I'll own that, stuff it in the pocket of my 501's and continue on. Why? Because GenX paid for this information in blood and bone and brain matter. But more importantly, the letters connected me with my boyz. And kids deserve connection. So do parents for that matter.

The letters also gave them insight as to why we're so grumpy.

GenX took the brunt of quantum leaps in technology, business practices and child-raising. We were forced, charged with, and expected to learn and adapt to every god-damned new piece of technological innovation that came down the line. It was friggin exhausting and non-stop. It made us grumpy and skeptical. Be Kind, Rewind, my ass.

Think of it this way. GenX's grandparents had ice and coal delivered to their houses by horse-cart and likely pooped in a hole out back if they didn't live in a city. So did everyone else for the previous 2500 years. Sure, generations before had growth in technology, but what we witnessed and assimilated has been unprecedented.

We've witnessed the entire space race from a hair-raising "Small step for mankind." to Shatner buying a ticket to outer space. I mean, come on now.

Our first cars were high-octane death traps and we had

"Speed Shops" dedicated to increasing that horsepower. Now they literally drive themselves and won't let you get hurt unless you're trying especially hard. We waited in line to play Space Invaders and stacked our quarters and lit cigarettes on the machine. Now there's Virtual Madden NFL in your living room and smoking's just about outlawed.

The countless flavors of cell phone we had to figure out over the years should earn us all immediate retirement. GenX had to learn and utilize every blessed version. All this happened after we had memorized scores of 7-digit phone numbers, road map directions and public transportation routes. We used cash and tokens and had to make change for christsakes. Then technology morphed every 6 months for the next 20 years and here we are.

Like I said, exhausting.

Mike has a postgraduate degree in Physics from Cambridge. Yeah, Issac Newton, Charles Darwin, Stephen Hawking Cambridge. Yet, he can't read an analog clock to save his life. Why? The same reason he doesn't have to memorize phone numbers. Progress.

So, when GenX hears folks boning about how their phone only holds 90 thousand pix, what a bitch it is to merge files, how their internet connection dropped twice yesterday, how WAZE sent them the wrong way, we sigh. Poor noobs.

We smell the White-Out. We hear echoes of the original AOL dial-up screech and inwardly shake our heads. We've been there. We've done that. We eventually learned how to make tech work for us, not vice versa.

We are the last generation who lived unleashed.

We've watched a device the size of a TI55 Calculator become a human appendage. It's cool, it's sparkly. But so was Rock 'Em Sock 'Em Robots. GenX knows. It'll morph, it'll grow, it'll disappear into something new.

The car made the world smaller. The airplane made the world smaller. The television made the world smaller. But our devices have made the world a 3"x 8" window where everyone has a platform and opinion and worst of all, an agenda.

We know the nonsense perpetrated on-line and in the popular media is not how life works.

A guy in the back wants my thoughts on the internet.

Well sir, in the interest of time, I'll keep it succinct.

85% of the internet is sparkly, Artificial Intelligence Generated lures built specifically to influence your actions and finances by parties unknown. 5% are unread emails from defunct accounts. The remaining 10% is like trying to find good pizza in Denver. A total waste of time and energy. I said what I said.

Thank you for the question.

Do I see this as incongruent with how I used the internet to keep my family connected? Not at all. I'll get sucked into a Family Guy click-bait maelstrom as quickly as the next dufus. Why? Because men and shiny stuff. That's why.

I believe, and GenX is with me, that the cacophony is too much. We are the first generation to have an Email address. We're the last generation to have lived without an Email address. We know it is not necessary. We know it is detrimental. So many people take what they see on-line as gospel. Our children need protection and adults need common sense to navigate the current digital world. Lures have hooks. As a fisherman, my scarred palms will bear testament.

We knew what weirdos and shit-bags looked like and how they operated and where they hung out. We even named them. We knew Buh. We knew Franky Dang Dang and Pete the Cleaners. We knew various flavors of motorcycle clubs and mob affiliates and the Shoplifting Dwarf Lady and the Black '54 Cadillac with black lace curtains in the windows, silently gliding down the alley at twilight full of gypsies.

Hell, my 2 classmates from high school grew up to fix NBA games for certain friends in NYC, got caught, paid their dues and wrote a book. Right, wrong or indifferent, gotta respect the entrepreneurial spirit and slick execution.

Our kids don't know this stuff. Why? Because today

everybody has artificial access to everybody and real access to nobody. In a world of screaming sound bites our kids need better information, real action items and a purpose more important than a thumbs-up in a post.

I'm a random boner and recognized my kids needed better information then they were getting from their myriad of outlets. They needed real information on how an adult behaves. They needed real information on how to recognize and stay out of harm's way.

They needed to know what it means to be a man in this world. Not an influencer, not a caricature, not a scared victim, not a bully, not a hysteric. A Man. We used to have a lot of them. Not so much these days.

I was lucky. I got my boys fresh out of the gate and through the efforts of so many real, live people, they are now responsible men making a positive impact on the world. They are leaving a legacy that won't be deleted by an algorithm for extra space. I'll say it again. The lovely and elusive Autumn my wife and I got lucky.

I gotta believe my letters were a small factor in how my boys came to reason out their decisions and actions. I believe they were helpful. I believe they may make their trip through life happier and more grounded. Grounded in the real.

And that's enough for an old Dad. Just enough.

Basta.

Thanks for listening.

"And all that is now,
And all that is gone,
And all that's to come,
And everything under the sun is in tune.
But the sun is eclipsed by the moon."

Eclipse – Pink Floyd, Dark Side of the Moon, 1973

Discography

- **The Bangles, Less Than Zero, 1987**
- **Beastie Boys, Hello Nasty, 1998**
- **Blondie, Eat to the Beat, 1979**
- **Blondie, Parallel Lines, 1978**
- **The Clash, Sandinista! 1980**
- **Phil Collins, Against All Odds, 1984**
- **Denis Leary, No Cure for Cancer, 1992**
- **Dire Straits, Making Movies, 1980**
- **Dire Straits, Brothers in Arms, 1985**
- **Duran Duran, Arena, 1984**
- **The Eurythmics, Be Yourself Tonight, 1985**
- **Eagles, Eagles, 1972**
- **The Fixx, Live in Concert, 1982**
- **Grover Washington, Jr., Winelight, 1980**
- **Genesis, Invisible Touch, 1987**
- **Heart, Tell It Like It Is, 1981**
- **Kris Kristofferson, The Silver-Tongued Devil and I, 1971**
- **John Lennon, Double Fantasy Stripped Down, 1981**
- **Missing Persons, Spring Session M, 1982**
- **Terry Jacks, Seasons in the Sun, 1973**
- **Tommy Makem, The Makem & Clancy Concert, 1977**
- **Pat Benatar, Crimes of Passion, 1980**
- **Pink Floyd, Dark Side of the Moon, 1973**
- **The Police, Ghost in the Machine, 1981**
- **The Pogues, Peace and Love, 1989**

- The Pogues, Rum, Sodomy and the Lash, 1980
- Public Enemy, Fear of a Black Planet, 1989
- R.E.M., Document, 1987
- Riders in the Sky, Cowboy Songs, 1996
- Diana Ross, To Love Again, 1981
- Stevie Ray Vaughan, Soul to Soul, 1985
- Tiffany, I Think We're Alone Now, 1984
- Twisted Sister, Stay Hungry, 1984
- Queen, Queen II, 1974
- The Vapors, New Clear Days, 1980
- Tom Waits, Heartattack and Vine, 1980
- Thomas Dolby, The Golden Age of Wireless, 1982

About the Author

Patrick McLaughlin is a happily married father of 2 grown boys. This simple sentence neatly encompasses 40 years of partnership and every brain damaging event that comes with raising boys from broken limbs to getting punched in the pants.

A GenX, 35-year professional headhunter recently retired, Patrick has deep people experience and a necessary knack for the humorous. He delves into his analog years highlighting life lessons with poignancy and sometimes biting commentary to his boys and now to a society that needs to listen.

www.ingramcontent.com/pod-product-compliance
Lightning Source LLC
Chambersburg PA
CBHW051230130726
47988CB00001B/294